KINGDOM GROWTH

80P

KINGDOM GROWTH

Changes, Journeys and Passion

Dominic Smart

Authentic

MILTON KEYNES ● COLORADO SPRINGS ● HYDERABAD

14 13 12 11 10 09 08   8 7 6 5 4 3 2 1

This edition published 2008 by Authentic Media
9 Holdom Avenue, Bletchley, Milton Keynes, MK1 1QR, UK
1820 Jet Stream Drive, Colorado Springs, CO 80921, USA
OM Authentic Media, Medchal Road, Jeedimetla Village,
Secunderabad 500 055, A.P., India
www.authenticmedia.co.uk

Authentic Media is a division of IBS-STL U.K., limited by guarantee, with its
Registered Office at Kingstown Broadway, Carlisle, Cumbria CA3 0HA.
Registered in England & Wales No. 1216232. Registered charity 270162

British Library Cataloguing in Publication Data
A catalogue record for this book is available from the British Library

ISBN-13: 978-1-85078-742-6

Cover Design by fourninezero design.
Print Management by Adare
Printed in Great Britain by J.H. Haynes & Co., Sparkford

Contents

Introduction

You might want to skip this bit

(On the other hand . . .)

If you've read *Kingdom Builders*,[1] which is concerned with Peter, Stephen and Philip, then you'll already know what this bit is about. It's about being God's fellow-builders and the book of Acts. So you might as well turn over the next few pages now and pick up the story from where we left it: with Philip's remarkable experience of God working in him so that he, like all the other fellow-builders in Acts, might do the works of God.

On the other hand, if you haven't read *Kingdom Builders* or, heaven forbid, you have but you've forgotten what it was about, you'd better read on.

The thinking

The book of Acts is not a manual of neat techniques for church growth. For sure, God does give a very clear indication that the church grows through the proclamation of the gospel in the power of his Holy Spirit. But beyond that, there's not much to copy. The book of the Acts of the Apostles, volume 2 of Luke's work, isn't written like an

instruction book. It lacks the proverb-like sayings or rid-
dles or instructions that we find in the wisdom literature
of the Old Testament: Proverbs, for instance. Neither is it
a legal document, like Leviticus. Nor did Luke write
exhortations to do this or commands to do that, as Paul
frequently did in his letters.

Acts is a story – it's narrative. Like all compelling stories, it's driven along by the plot-line and the characters.
Dramatic events are interspersed with historical 'book-
marks': reference points that make it clear that it's not to
be read as a fable but to be taken seriously as an account
of what actually happened.

The plot, of course, is God's. It unfolds the progress of
the mission of God as it extends from the Old Testament
into the 'gospel years' in which we live – the years
between Christ's ascension and his return. The dramatic
events, of which there are many in this page-turner of a
story, are events that God orchestrated and in which he
shows both his wisdom and his power. As God moves
history along the lines of his purpose, we see a mix of
coincidences and supernatural incidents that reveal his
sovereign hand.

So it's the story of God's work to progress his mission,
to redeem sinners and to extend the Kingdom of his
Christ, his anointed King and beloved Son. This makes
the characters crucial to any understanding of the book,
and to what we hear it saying to us. Acts is the story of
what God did in the lives of men and women in order to
build his Kingdom. Principally, it's the story of what he
did in the lives of those through whom, and with whom,
he was doing the building. It's about God and his people
rather than about the church and its programmes. What
did God do with and in people so that they could do his
works, works which extend and mirror those of the one
true Kingdom-Builder, the King himself, Jesus the Christ?

That question lies at the heart of these two volumes and at the heart of how to read Acts. Don't read it like a car repair manual: 'Do this, then that, then the other, and your car will work.' You'll be grossly disappointed because you simply won't be able to do most of what's written there. Instead, look at what God did through his people, in this case Saul of Tarsus who became Paul, the Apostle to the Gentiles, and ask, 'What did God have to do in his life so that he became a fellow-builder?' Then follow through with the next question: 'Will I be ready for him to do the same kind of thing – though probably in different ways – in my life?'

It immediately prompts us to ask what God is doing in our lives. There is a way of looking at the whole of life which constantly assumes that God is at work for his glory, for the good of the church, for the spread of the gospel and for our growth in his grace. That's the basic assumption: he is at work in everything for precisely these purposes. Having that as the starting point, we read our situations with the expectation that God is constantly and actively progressing our lives, not occasionally involved as an over-active spectator who cannot help but interfere from time to time. So how is he using the enforced rest after your car crash in order to engage you more deeply and fruitfully in the building of his Kingdom? Assume that he is; look for how. How is he at work in you now that your wife is having chemotherapy for breast cancer? How is he at work, for these purposes, in your job promotion? How is he working in you so that you can do the works of God? What is he training you to be through your new friends at the slimming club (less envious), your daughter's exams (more patient!), your Pastor's preaching (same again), your colleague's annoying habit of interrupting you (a more truthful colleague)? What is he doing in you so that you are more aligned with his building work? And what is he teaching you to expect as his Kingdom advances over the earth via your life? It's not a self-preoccupied way of reading Acts, because the focus of the question is on the building of God's Kingdom rather than on your own personal sanctification and satisfaction.

What is he doing in your life for the sake of his Son?

In this second volume, we look at a few (and only a few – this doesn't aim to be comprehensive) incidents in the life of this remarkably gifted and powerful character, whom we have already encountered at the stoning of Stephen. Saul of Tarsus was weak and formidable, kind and tempestuous, brave and needy, single-minded yet widely compassionate, full of life yet always bearing Christ's death in his own body. What did God have to do in his life to make him, and make him a better, Kingdom-builder? Are you ready for him to do the same kind of thing in your life?

1

The most unlikely man on earth

or

Why God's ways aren't ours

Recruitment and selection are fascinating processes for a company to negotiate. What does the job that we're advertising involve: what are the tasks and working relationships? What sort of person are we looking for, and how do we go about finding them? What are the critical criteria to apply as we filter the CVs that will be sent? What do we want to see when we interview? How do we entice strong applicants?

It is like that in every kind of business, including the construction industry. If the world's big builders take their work so seriously, how much more important to use the very best recruitment and selection practices when what's being built is the Kingdom of God! Surely?

Well, perhaps not.

Our assumptions about people's suitability for the post of God's fellow-builder are often best viewed upside down. For a start, we are never in charge of the recruitment process. We are all recruited by the One who directs the whole building work, and whose ability and zeal guarantee its success. Secondly, we don't define success – God does. Thirdly, we tend to look for people who are already suitable because although we can provide training, we can't fundamentally change people. God's mission is to do both, but do them the other way round – first the fundamental change, then the training. So he can choose anyone he wants to choose. Fourthly, there is a dimension to God's building work that hasn't quite penetrated the human resources departments of most companies yet: God is God and we aren't. He is not accountable to his fellow-workers, or in fact to anyone. He is our Maker, not our employer, who made us for a close and loving relationship with himself. He is holy and is concerned not simply to get jobs done but with the holiness of his fellow-workers. He is the one true recipient of all the earth's glory and will bring maximum glory to his own name – our destiny is to be enabled to glorify him as we ought.

Who would you have chosen?

Nowhere in the biblical account of the increase of God's Kingdom does the difference between our way of choosing people for a job and God's way become more apparent than with Saul of Tarsus. There can hardly be a clearer example than this of God's ways not being ours. There can hardly be a greater distinction between the wisdom of God and the wisdom of people, than in the conversion and calling of the most calculating and vicious enemy of the church. He was the most unlikely man on earth.

The story so far

Before we launch into Acts chapter 9, we need to step back from the details and take note of the flow of what's happening in the life of God's church. We can take it back to the gospels.

As Jesus turned towards Jerusalem and the cross, he stated his intention to build his church (Mt. 16:18). He included in the building process those who would be his disciples, when he gave commands that come in the form of commissions: statements about a mission that is shared (hence 'commissions') between the One who sends and those who are sent. The most celebrated of these is commonly called the Great Commission (Mt. 28:16–20). Jesus' commissions form part of a description of God's mission that stretches from before time to the end of time – from eternity to eternity. Those who receive the commissions are supported with a massive promise, when after his resurrection Jesus says to the assembled disciples they will receive power when the Holy Spirit comes upon them; then they will be his witnesses in Jerusalem, Judea, Samaria and to the ends of the earth (Acts 1:8). The Spirit is poured out on the church at Pentecost and from that moment the gospel begins to spread. It quickly engulfs Jerusalem, but how is it to spread to the other places? Especially, how is the gospel going to be the means by which God will reach the Gentiles – 'the nations'? That had been his declared intention for centuries, but how would it get to them?

The door to the Gentile world has been opened a little before Saul becomes a servant of the gospel. Already, the persecution of believers in Jerusalem following Stephen's death has dispersed the church into the further reaches of the Jewish world (Acts 8:1). Philip has seen great results as he has 'proclaimed the Christ' in Samaria (Acts 8:5–8).

From the city in Samaria he is called to the middle of nowhere to meet, as it turns out, the best possible missionary to the Ethiopians – the Ethiopian chancellor of the exchequer. The promise that God will reach Gentiles is about to receive fresh fulfilment as well. In Acts 10, only a few verses after Saul's conversion, Peter will proclaim the Christ to a Gentile centurion in Caesarea and a kind of Caesarean Pentecost will happen. The promise of the church's numerical and geographical growth is advancing, but Peter's visit into the Gentile world was only that – a visit. There are still 'the ends of the earth' to reach. Who will go further and who will go repeatedly? Who will be in it for the long haul? Who will do the deeply cross-cultural mission? The mission of God, which is the source of the church's life and the command over the church's work, demands that workers lift up their eyes to God's more distant harvest fields. But who will devote themselves under the call of God to take the gospel over such vast physical, cultural and religious distances, into the world of the Gentiles?

Who would your church leaders choose? Form a search committee. Set up the job criteria, advertise the post, scan the applications. Who would you choose to take the gospel of the Lord Jesus Christ, along with other Christians, with accountability to the apostles and other church leaders in Jerusalem, and at immense personal cost, to the Gentile world?

Probably not Saul of Tarsus.

Probably not the man who stood watching as Stephen was stoned to death. Probably not the man who, as Luke introduces him at the beginning of Acts 9, 'was still breathing out murderous threats against the Lord's disciples' (9:1).

Look at how he described himself later when, writing to the church in Galatia, he looked back on what God has taught him: 'For you have heard of my previous way of life in Judaism, how intensely I persecuted the church of God and tried to destroy it' (Gal. 1:13).

We tend to get a picture of Saul that is filtered through our readings of his letters. We think of the missionary and theologian with a pastor's heart and huge courage for the sake of the gospel. But the pre-conversion Saul was worse than I suspect we tend to see him as being. His avowed intention was to destroy the church, which ranks him alongside the worst of persecutors in the history of the church. He was not just out to give a few Christians a hard time somewhere because he didn't like them. His very considerable energy was focused on wiping out the entire church, on killing the body of Christ.

Look at what he said in Acts 22:4–5: 'I persecuted the followers of this Way to their death, arresting both men and women and throwing them into prison, as also the high priest and all the Council can testify.' Again, Acts 26:9–11

> I too was convinced that I ought to do all that was possible to oppose the name of Jesus of Nazareth. And that is just what I did in Jerusalem. On the authority of the chief priests I put many of the saints in prison, and when they were put to death, I cast my vote against them. Many a time I went from one synagogue to another to have them punished, and I tried to force them to blaspheme. In my obsession against them, I even went to foreign cities to persecute them.

Would you have chosen that man to work with other believers?

And what about taking the gospel to Gentiles? He describes himself as 'circumcised on the eighth day, of the people of Israel, of the tribe of Benjamin, a Hebrew of Hebrews; in regard to the law, a Pharisee; as for zeal, persecuting the church; as for legalistic righteousness, faultless' (Phil. 3:5–6). He hated Gentiles. He had been schooled in a background that regarded Gentiles as fuel for the fires of Hades, and taught that Gentiles were like dogs: so vile that you'd steer well clear of them. If he touched a Gentile he would be ceremonially unclean and unable to come to God because, so the reasoning went, God also hated Gentiles.

Would you have chosen this man for a life of hardship and suffering – not least through persecution by his fel-low-Jews? He was among the elite of Jewish society, a Pharisee of the highest order. He was educated. He com-manded people, generating fear and respect. He was a privileged member of society. Ask him to suffer? I don't think we would.

Chiefly, would we pick him to carry the gospel of the name of Jesus Christ? Take note of what he wrote in Acts 26:9: 'I too was convinced that I ought to do all that was possible to oppose the name of Jesus of Nazareth.'

When Saul is making his way to Damascus later in chapter 9, Jesus asks him 'Saul, Saul, why do you perse-cute me?' We often take that to mean that Jesus feels the attacks on the church in Jerusalem personally. The per-secution targeted the Christians and Jesus so closely identifies with them that it's 'as if' he was being perse-cuted. But in Saul's mind there's no 'as if'. Saul was tar-geting Jesus himself – his name, his reputation and his influence. Saul hated the idea that the name of Jesus of Nazareth should be the name of the Messiah.

As far as Saul was concerned, the name of Jesus was bad news: theologically, because the idea that Jesus who had been crucified could be the Messiah was repulsive; socially, because the Christians were a threat to the social order exerted by the Sanhedrin, the Jewish ruling council; and politically, because the power-brokers of Jewish society and the enforcers of the Jewish 'truth regime' – the Sanhedrin, the Pharisees, and the teachers of the law – were all opposed by Jesus' followers in the name of Jesus. Saul was convinced that he ought to aim his hatred straight at Jesus. And Jesus knew it.

So how likely a candidate was Saul for the job of proclaiming the good news about Jesus Christ?

The CV would have to say that the applicant was a committed racist, intellectually opposed to Christianity and full of personal hatred towards Christ, with a track record second to none when it came to liquidating Christians. Church annihilation, not growth, was his avowed intent.

And yet, as God is going to say to Ananias in Damascus, 'This man is my chosen instrument to carry my name before the Gentiles' (9:15).

Do you see what I mean about Acts not being so much a manual to follow as a theological story about God? No one in their right mind would choose Saul. It would be like choosing a ravenous wolf for the post of sheepdog. We would be right not to consider Saul. But we would be wrong to say that God couldn't choose Saul. We would be wrong to say that this or that person, whom we accurately perceive to be a vile enemy of the gospel, could not become its most significant servant in our town or any town. We would be wrong to tell God who he could choose as his instrument.

Why? Because as a simple matter of fact God did choose this man Saul; and because God has enough grace to love his enemies (after all, the blood of Jesus Christ covers his enemies' sins) and because Christ's Lordship extends over his enemies as well as over those who acknowledge his sovereignty.

There's one more thing: when we choose, our wisdom is glorified. But God's chief concern is not for our glory: it's for his own glory. Who gains the most glory in what we are about to study? Not the early church, for a bold and radical appointment, but God, for his wisdom and grace.

And how would you have persuaded this person?

As we read the Bible, we discern basic principles about how we should approach other people – courtesy, true and loving speech (both, notice), integrity, humility, compassion, wisdom and so on. Yet God seems to be breaking the rule book all the time.

We soon learn that, in most walks of life, the approach is everything; from romance to rock climbing; from a visit to the doctor to a quiet word with the referee or the vicar. When we suspect that tact and diplomacy might be required, we become doubly careful.

How does God approach those whom he wishes to recruit? The simple but far from easy answer is that he approaches them as God. The 'God-ness of God' is always a challenge to us. The unpredictability of the Master-Builder is constantly disconcerting yet joyously brilliant. We can never assume that he's going to handle people in ways that we can either foresee or mimic. He takes the initiative with breathtakingly creative genius that leaves us constantly catching up with him. Often it leaves us with the profoundly disturbing task of accepting that he has worked, and that he is God. Much of the troubling of our souls that we experience when we see the work of God in a person or a fellowship – or for that matter in national and international life – is at heart a matter of accepting that God is God.

So how does God do it? (You might want to read Acts 9:1–32 at this point.) First, he sends a flash of light so bright that Saul is blinded. (It will take a miraculous intervention to restore it again.) Then God floors him. (Dignified Saul grovels in the dust, publicly.) Then there's a theophany. (A speech from heaven: in the Old Testament, Saul's thought-shaping Scripture, they almost always cause fear and dread.) Jesus pins him to the ground with a non-negotiable accusation wrapped up as an unanswerable question.

Saul finds himself responding to the question with another question. It's debatable whether or not he would have been aware of how vital his response is, but the identity of the One he calls 'Lord' is in fact the pivotal question in Saul's entire life. Then, after Jesus the Messiah has answered the question and repeated the charge against Saul, he does exactly the thing that the One who really is Lord would do: he commands him with life-changing power and authority.

Just like that.

In almost no time at all, with no warning and, as far as we know, in response to no one's prayers, Jesus Christ has converted the church's worst enemy. He has taken him from being a servant of Satan to being a servant of Jesus Christ; slave will be his own preferred word later. In that brief encounter, the course of the man's entire life has been turned round. He is led by the hand into the city where his one plan was to destroy the church; he has been violently assaulted by the Lord of grace and now finds himself in need of that very church. The one who lost his sight and was verbally accosted by Christ becomes, immediately, a praying visionary whose careful plans have been replaced with the command simply to wait for further instructions.

Saul is not the man we would have chosen; we wouldn't have brought him into the Kingdom and its work in this way; we couldn't have made such a transformation in his life.

But it is the privilege of the fellow-builders to watch God at work.

Our challenge is to recover our faith and our joy in this somewhat wild work of God, instead of yawning on the plateau of predictability. We see new ways of reaching our communities with the gospel or of singing praise; perhaps we are reinvigorated by new leadership in the fellowship or by a new way of praying. But after a frighteningly short period of excitement, we reach a plateau. The novelty has worn off. The flower arranging, skate park, evangelistic tea dance and the bucking bronco evening with speaker: all become part of the furniture again and the building of his Kingdom becomes predictable. It falls under our control. We assume that we can and ought to manage it. On such a plateau, we can soon become either bored or complacent. The danger then is that we seek some fresh spiritual novelty, as if 'buzz' could satisfy our souls. It can't, but a greater vision of God can because he can satisfy our souls. His power, his inventiveness, his grace, his purposes and new directions – these can satisfy our souls and refresh our faith. New ideas are fine (though the bucking bronco might take a bit of selling to the church leaders) but a more realistic and less predictive appreciation of the One who is Lord can improve our attitude to the building work in a way that no 'latest thing' ever can. One leads to adoration and worship – the other leads to the current bandwagon. One leads to humility, the other to the smugness of those with the latest spiritual gadget. One leads to day-by-day trust, the other leads to mere restlessness.

What would our churches be like if we genuinely did live by faith in the God who builds his Kingdom even by the most extraordinary means? It would be scary to begin with but ultimately it would be less of a strain. It would also revive our praying: we would have a greater sense of our need. The answers to those prayers would build our faith yet more and cause greater thanksgiving to rise to God's name. Our God will constantly disrupt our patterns of activity and our limited expectations as his government increases. He is the same God as he was on the road to Damascus. He is still doing the same building work and he still blows apart all the neat compartments that we so quickly construct and into which we are so prone to try to tidy him.

2

The call

Six details of the call

We've taken account of the fact that God chooses Saul and of the way in which he calls Saul. Both reflect God's plans and power, not the church's. What about the details of the call itself? What's actually happening?

This transformation clearly bears the fingerprint of God's work. There are six details that I want us to notice.

1. It's a personal encounter

Saul meets a person. He is not simply persuaded to think differently nor is he merely stimulated to have new emotions. He does not sign up for membership of a new institution nor does he just embark on a new job. Many changes of this ilk do take place but they are all a consequence of the personal encounter with the Messiah.

God is not a behavioural engineer who merely changes conduct. His work is both deeper and more relational than that. He regards us with love; he is faithful. He is the Father and we share the life of the Son. The

Spirit who unites us with the Son can be caused to grieve by us. These are all relational categories. We worship one God in three Persons who has made us to reflect his image. We are made for relationships and largely defined by them. Thus a lack of relationships creates the biggest void and the most insatiable restlessness that the human heart can know. The problem is greatest when it comes to the relationship with God. When St Augustine prayed 'You have created us for yourself and our hearts are restless until they find their rest in you', he was touching on one of the most basic and God-intended needs of humanity.

Up until now, Saul has not met Jesus. His followers, yes. The apostles' teaching and the proclamation of the gospel, yes. But so far, the One he has opposed so bitterly has just been a name, a figure who others have met. Not any longer. Jesus, in person, addresses Saul in person. Man to man, in fact God to man. We ought not to underestimate the shock of this to someone who has assumed that the resurrection didn't happen. As far as Saul is concerned, the events that recently rocked Jerusalem – miracles, preaching, mass conversions and the like – have only involved the people that he can see, the followers of 'The Way'. Suddenly he is confronted by one he assumed to be dead but who is very much alive. And it turns out that he has been present and active in all the seismic shocks that have hit his religion. The church is not simply a rebellious insurrectionist movement. It has God behind it. And where does that leave the religious leaders who, like Saul, thought that they were doing God's will in crucifying Christ and attempting to destroy the church?

God really does turn Saul's world upside-down. What he thought was bad is good. What he has always held to be true is false. What he had opposed with unequalled zeal was the truth. The One he thought was a blasphemous man is God. This deep impact comes through a personal encounter with God; not through a heated discussion or a calm exchange of clever ideas but in a person-to-person meeting with Christ.

This is a basic element in the process by which people are called from darkness to light. One way or another, they are led to the Son by the Father through the Spirit. Saul writes about it much later in his life when he teaches the church in Rome. He reasoned with them about the way in which his own people, the Jews, might come to see that Jesus is the inner meaning and the end-point of what we now call the Old Testament. In Romans 10 he asks a series of questions that take us along the pathway to calling on the name of the Lord and being saved. 'How, then, can they call on the one they have not believed in? And how can they believe in the one of whom they have not heard? And how can they hear without someone preaching to them? And how can they preach unless they are sent?' (Rom. 10:14–15). That second question, 'And how can they believe in the one of whom they have not heard?' is mistranslated in most English versions of the New Testament. The problem is that the 'of whom' isn't actually there in the Greek. As Charles Cranfield points out in his commentary on Romans, Saul is not saying that the hearers hear a message about Christ, but rather 'the thought is of their hearing Christ speaking in the message of the preachers'.[2] He knew what he was talking about. It had happened to him on the road to Damascus.

When we speak the message, Christ speaks through us. A personal encounter takes place, which leaves no one unaltered. Towards him or away from him, people are moved by hearing Christ, even if, like Saul, they don't know the identity of the One to whom or against whom they respond.

So when we pray for the communication of the gospel, in whatever situation and in whatever style it's being done, we need to be clear in our own minds about what's happening. Pray that the message is proclaimed faithfully, and that the hearers hear Christ making a personal address to them. Pray for a personal encounter initiated by the living Lord. We can pray that in Jesus' name because that is just what Jesus does. As Saul discovered.

2. Christ deals with a relationship broken by sin

Saul of Tarsus would have denied that he had any kind of relationship at all with Jesus of Nazareth. He would have been wrong. He could not escape having a relationship with Jesus for two reasons. The first is that Jesus is Saul's Maker.

The Maker and all that he has made

The creature–Creator relationship is a given – the quality of it can change, but the fact of it can't. Everyone, everywhere, at all times, has this relationship with the Creator. It's forged from God's side. It's one that he constitutes as he makes all things and makes them for his glory.

A few texts that speak of Jesus in this way will help us here: 'In the beginning was the Word, and the Word was with God, and the Word was God. He was with God in the beginning. Through him all things were made;

without him nothing was made that has been made'
(Jn.1:1–3).

Including Saul of Tarsus! He was to see it that way
himself later in his life. Under the inspiration of the
Spirit, he wrote to the church in Colosse: 'For by him all
things were created: things in heaven and on earth, visi-
ble and invisible, whether thrones or powers or rulers or
authorities; all things were created by him and for him'
(Col. 1:16).

Notice, *for* him. The intention for creation was for a
relationship with Jesus. Not in the sense that one day
such a relationship might be nice if it all works out okay,
but that from the beginning, all things were committed
to Jesus to serve and glorify their Maker.

Nor is that relationship confined to the origins of all
things. Jesus is the Creator who sustains all things – the
relationship is a constant. So Saul goes on to write: 'He
is before all things, and in him all things hold together'
(Col. 1:17).

The writer to the Hebrews makes the same points
about making and sustaining to his audience of converted Jews: '. . . in these last days he has spoken to us by his
Son, whom he appointed heir of all things, and through
whom he made the universe. The Son is the radiance of
God's glory and the exact representation of his being,
sustaining all things by his powerful word' (Heb. 1:2–3).

Notice that he adds a glimpse of the future: Jesus will
inherit all things. Past, present and future, all created
things are incapable of being described properly without talking about how they stand in relation to their
Creator.

Saul has been living as an antagonist – he has not
been neutral with reference to his Maker, but has been
in rebellion against him. It's a relationship, and it's one
marked by animosity and unbridled hostility from

Saul's side. 'Once you were alienated from God and were enemies in your minds because of your evil behaviour' (Col. 1:21). And wasn't it this very Creator who, as one of us, said 'He who is not with me is against me, and he who does not gather with me scatters' (Mt. 12: 30)?

It's crucial to have the fundamental hostility towards God on the part of sinners firmly in our minds as we engage in the work of God's fellow-builders. The Kingdom of God does not grow in a world that is friendly towards its Maker. Most of the people that we know hardly ever think about having a Maker, though many, if asked, might admit that there's 'something' there. But a personal God who made George in Sales and who made Annette who's having a great time at University and who made Rob the GP? Hardly, and anyway, what does it matter? Does it matter to Nazim, who seeks to arrange his own life his own way, that the One who made him and sustains him, loves him and has compassion on him? And what of Tom, whose success in the Army earned him high rank, a high pension and (he thinks) the moral high ground that comes from seeing scattered body parts and burned out tanks and who thinks that religion is the curse of humanity? Or Ricardo, who fiercely attacks the notion of a Creator God at every opportunity and celebrates his views that the heavens declare the glory of chance?

Are these people in a relationship with God?

Yes. Not because they have established it, but because God has established it by making them. What they have done is to turn it into a hostile relationship by their sin.

There is no neutrality. There's not an overcrowded fence: there isn't a fence.

The glorified Lord of all

The second reason why Saul can't escape having a relationship with Jesus is that Jesus is Lord of everything. A relationship exists between a king and his subject, whatever the subject thinks of his king. Like the Creator–creature relationship, it's a given.

In the most dramatic turnaround in history, the Man whom Saul's crowd had exerted all their power against and crucified was now their Lord. Peter had proclaimed it as clearly as it could possibly be said to the Sanhedrin and the rest of the Jewish establishment: 'Therefore let all Israel be assured of this: God has made this Jesus, whom you crucified, both Lord and Christ' (Acts 2:36).

There's irony for you! They thought that they had won. They thought that their power had prevailed over Jesus' power. Yet the very way that they chose to exert their supposed lordship over Jesus – the cross – was the very means by which Christ became Lord. It was the most stupendous own goal in history. They scored: God won!

George the rep, Annette the student, Rob, Nazim, Major Tom and Ricardo the atheist all have this second thing in common: Jesus Christ is their Lord. Not because they acknowledge him to be so but because the Father has made the Son Lord and Christ: King of everything. George and company are not (yet, perhaps) in his Kingdom, in that they do not yield to his kingship. But one day they will acknowledge that Jesus Christ is Lord. And up until that moment they will be under the governance of the all-providing Lord. The power of speech that they use to deny him is given to them by him. The bodies with which they live out their civilised rebellion against him are fed and clothed at the command of the King of all things. The minds with which they constantly reaffirm their self-rule and fashion their gods are supplied with blood and oxygen by the hand of the Lord of all things. This Lordship is his as a right, and as simple matter of fact, and is exercised by him from a throne gained by way of a cross. Their Creator is their Redeemer-King. They might not want to believe it, but so what? Since when has Jesus been merely what people want to believe him to be?

Saul's relation to the Lord was one of sinful rebellion – kicking against him all the time. As with Christ the Creator, so with Christ the Lord: there is no neutrality.

Does that seem strange to us? That Jesus is Lord of those who are his enemies? Don't we have, as a part of our evangelical background, the supposedly self-evident truth that 'if we don't make him Lord of all he's not Lord at all'? But that's not what the Bible teaches! He is Lord of all his enemies. Recall the encounter that Jesus had with his worst enemy, Satan. In the wilderness, in the burning heat and the hunger and dryness, the question of who is Lord becomes one of the central issues. Read these exchanges that are part of the second and third temptations

> Then the devil took him to the holy city and had him stand on the highest point of the temple. 'If you are the Son of God,' he said, 'throw yourself down. For it is written: "He will command his angels concerning you, and they will lift you up in their hands, so that you will not

strike your foot against a stone."' Jesus answered him, 'It is also written: "Do not put *the Lord your God* to the test."' Again, the devil took him to a very high mountain and showed him all the kingdoms of the world and their splendour. 'All this I will give you,' he said, 'if you will bow down and worship me.' Jesus said to him, 'Away from me, Satan! For it is written: "*Worship the Lord your God, and serve him only*"' (Mt. 4:5–10: my italics).

God's worst enemy is under the Lordship of the Anointed One. He always has been and always will be. That's why he's God's enemy: he can't stand someone other than himself being enthroned over all things and especially over him.

3. It's a call to share in the growth of God's Kingdom

Is Saul converted for Saul's sake?

Not entirely. God doesn't save people for their sakes alone.

Recall what Jesus had said to the disciples: 'You did not choose me, but I chose you and appointed you to go and bear fruit – fruit that will last. Then the Father will give you whatever you ask in my name' (Jn. 15:16).

Saul has been chosen to be God's instrument for ful-filling the commission that he gave to the disciples back in Acts 1:8. Jerusalem, Judea and Samaria were covered. But out into Gentile territory – the ends of the earth – was going to be Saul's remit . . . 'The Lord said to Ananias "This man is my chosen instrument to carry my name before the Gentiles and their kings and before the people of Israel. I will show him how much he must suf-fer for my name"' (Acts 9:15–16).

That is the summary of the rest of Saul's life. As C.H. Spurgeon once said, 'Every Christian is either a missionary or an impostor.' Saul's conversion will take him into the presence of Gentiles and their kings. It will involve him in witnessing to the Jews that Jesus is the Messiah. It will cause him suffering and cost him his life.

Just like Jesus, then.

What a difference it makes when we grasp this aspect of God's work in the lives of his fellow-builders.

Our sinful minds have always tended to be self-centred. The culture that we live in reinforces that innate tendency every day: look out for number one; blow your own trumpet (even if it's in a rather muted British way) because nobody else will; buy this – 'because you're worth it'. But this self-absorbed life is neither what we were made for nor what Christ gave himself on the cross to save us for. As we've already noted, we weren't made for ourselves, but for God. The first question in *The Longer Catechism of the Westminster Confession* (not, it has to be said, everyone's favourite Christian read these days) asks 'What is the chief end of man?' The answer is 'To glorify God and enjoy him for ever.'

Our culture teaches us to act as if the very opposite were true: God's chief end is to glorify us and empower us to enjoy ourselves for ever. This reversal affects our praying (fervent when seeking a parking place), our reaction to church (didn't 'do it' for me this morning), and among myriad other aspects of life, our overwhelming idea of why God saves us (I'm the biggest thing on his mind). But God's main reason was rightly and properly himself. His glory, his creation purposes, his victory over that which opposed him, his honour in the heavenly places as well as on the earth, his missionary purpose to redeem a worshipping people from all nations – these lie at the heart of our salvation. What a blessing! You were made and re-made for purposes bigger than yourself. He didn't convert you for purposes that extend only as far as your own blissful eternity. He called you and cleansed you from your sin primarily so that he might commission you to be a fellow-builder with him of an eternal city.

> What we think that we are converted for will make a profound difference to how we live with God. If we think that we've been converted primarily for our sakes, we'll tend to live as if God is primarily with us to serve us. But if we have grasped that he gave us new life primarily for his sake, then our life with God will be very different. It will tend to be a conversation in which, rather than us saying to God 'for my sake', we hear God saying to us 'for *my* sake.'

4. It involves being filled with the Holy Spirit

Notice what happens when Ananias goes to meet Saul: 'Ananias went to the house and entered it. Placing his hands on Saul, he said, "Brother Saul, the Lord – Jesus, who appeared to you on the road as you were coming here – has sent me so that you may see again and be filled with the Holy Spirit"' (Acts 9:17).

Why? Because Saul was going to become a witness. Conversion gives a person a testimony. Teaching gives a person a message. Love gives a person a motive. It is only the indwelling Spirit who gives us power. Recall how Jesus delayed the disciples from going out on their missionary work until they had God's power to do it.

> 'This is what is written: The Christ will suffer and rise from the dead on the third day, and repentance and

forgiveness of sins will be preached in his name to all
nations, beginning at Jerusalem. You are witnesses of
these things. I am going to send you what my Father
has promised; but stay in the city until you have been
clothed with power from on high' (Lk. 24:46–49).

Later, he tells them again that it is God's power that
makes them his witnesses: '. . . you will receive power
when the Holy Spirit comes on you; and you will be my
witnesses in Jerusalem, and in all Judea and Samaria,
and to the ends of the earth' (Acts 1:8).

It was absolutely necessary that if Saul was to be a fellow-builder, he should be filled with the Holy Spirit.
Such filling is repetitive, continuously going on in the
lives of God's servants in Acts. For both Peter and
Stephen, when God engineered the occasion for bold,
penetrating witness, the Spirit filled them so that they
could rise to the moment and share in the building of the
Kingdom. It was going to be no different for Saul and it
will be no different for you and me.

5. It requires courageous companions: Ananias and the assassin's apartment

The point of looking so closely at Saul's conversion is to
see that in order to be a co-worker with God, we need to
have total respect for God's outrageously unconven-
tional wisdom. Despite our fears or our expectations
that 'normality' ought always to prevail, we work with
the great I AM and must be prepared to accept the odd
surprise along the way.

Which brings us to a devout man who was asked by
God to go to the assassin's apartment. It's interesting to
see how Ananias is so willing to have this encounter

with Saul: 'In Damascus there was a disciple named Ananias. The Lord called to him in a vision, "Ananias!" "Yes, Lord," he answered.' There is an immediate willingness in Ananias' heart. Before he knows what the call is going to be, he answers 'Yes, Lord.' The two words belong together, do they not: 'Yes' and 'Lord'? If you know who he is, and you acknowledge it for yourself so that with new instincts you call him 'Lord', what other word in all the world's vocabularies is going to be more appropriate than 'Yes'?

Ananias' responsiveness is crucial to the whole purpose. Without Ananias being there and being the kind of man who immediately jumps to obey, the whole thing wouldn't have progressed. We can argue predestination and free will until the cows come home, but God put Ananias there and then in order to fulfil his word. The same thing had happened earlier in Acts with Philip. God had said that he would have witnesses in Samaria. He needed Philip to be the kind of man who would speak of Christ wherever he went, so that having being thrown out of Jerusalem and finding himself in Samaria, he bears witness to the Lord Jesus Christ.

Is God risking the whole venture on Ananias getting it right? No, not really. For God, who needed Ananias, made Ananias what he needed him to be. This devout observer of the law had become a man of grace. Unlike so many of his fellow-Israelites, he had accepted that Jesus was the Messiah. The Father who had opened the eyes of Peter in Caesarea to see and say 'You are the Christ, the son of the living God', had done just the same in Damascus with Ananias. Just as God gives what he commands, so he creates whatever he needs. We pray with David in Psalm 51, 'Create in me a pure heart, O God.' How vital that we also learn to pray 'Create in me a willing heart, O Lord.' And he will, though what he might ask us to do in order to demonstrate his handiwork might be the last thing on earth that we would naturally have wanted to do.

So Ananias is called, willingly says 'Yes' and then the Lord tells him what to do: 'Go to the house of Judas on Straight Street . . .'

(Isn't that a great name for a street? You can't help being amused by the irony that Saul, whose twisted, crooked life has been set right by God, is now waiting on Straight Street.)

'. . . ask for a man from Tarsus named Saul, for he is praying. In a vision he has seen a man named Ananias come and place his hands on him to restore his sight' (Acts 9:11–12). God had given Saul the vision.

> 'Lord,' Ananias answered, 'I have heard many reports about this man and all the harm he has done to your saints in Jerusalem. And he has come here . . . [obviously the believers in Damascus knew that Saul was on his way] . . . with authority from the chief priest to arrest all who call on your name.'
>
> But the Lord said to Ananias, 'Go! This man is my chosen instrument to carry my name before the Gentiles and their kings and before the people of Israel. I will show him how much he must suffer for my name' (Acts 9:13–16).

Did Ananias really understand the whole picture? Or did he make his way through the streets and alleys of Damascus to meet the deadly assassin, bewildered at what he found himself doing? I suspect the latter.

Many times God calls us to go and speak to people without us having a clue as to how it will turn out. We are bewildered, but we know that we have to go and speak to this person here or that person there. We don't know if they are going to respond, but we have had such a nudge from God that we know that we've got to invite Jim and his partner for dinner, even though we might be apprehensive about the evening. Or we know we've got to go along to that leaving party for George from Sales, even though we are not natural party animals. Slightly bewildered, we still obey the God who seems to feel no compelling obligation to explain everything to our satisfaction. He rarely presents us with a watertight business plan, like the ones that we might have to present to a bank manager as we seek permission for a new venture. But then he's not applying to us for resources to build his Kingdom. So we obey, not knowing the outcome. Doing so is part of the faith that he gives us. By faith, we let the current of God's missionary love and the wind of his Spirit direct us. We release our grip on the tiller; we yield control to God; we refuse our fears.

6. It's the work of the Sovereign Saviour

So Ananias went to the house and placed his hands on Saul. And there, as we have read, Saul is baptised, takes some food, regains his strength and spends several days with the disciples in Damascus. At once he begins to preach in the synagogues. But there is a final element of Saul's conversion that we need to dwell on, just to get the astounding sovereignty of God embedded in our minds. It has two dimensions in Saul's story.

We can't second-guess God!

We really can't. We don't know what on earth he's going to do next with those who are willing and able, like Ananias, nor with those who are unwilling and unable, like Saul. The cliché is that 'God can only steer a rolling stone.' It's a phrase that helpfully reminds us that God guides those who are actively walking with him, rather than those who have mastered the dubious calling to be couch-potatoes for Christ. But like most clichés, it masks truth as well as reminding us of it. God is not confined to steering stones that happen to be joyously rolling around his Kingdom when he needs one. God can get a stone rolling in the first place. Patently so, since he did it with Saul and has done it with you and me. We cannot dictate to him what he can do next or in whose life he can do it. Had we been on the early church's search committee, we would probably have got it hopelessly wrong (or more disturbingly, hopelessly 'right' in terms of conventional wisdom). If we'd been having a committee meeting in Damascus we would probably have chosen Ananias, the most likely man. But God's chosen instrument for reaching Gentiles was the most unlikely man on earth.

There's a particular edge to this at the moment. In the name of wisdom, our church leaders are being enticed by no end of boldly marketed management techniques that cry out to overworked leaders. 'Seven of this, Pastor.' 'Try twenty-one of these, Vicar.' 'Buy this bunch of eleven practical steps to a successful church.' The books and brochures shout out their confident claims to be able to deliver what every keen Christian leader properly wants to see. For sure, wisdom is a make-happen quality that we need in large quantities. But we do not gain it from the noise and clamour of brash ideas for mastering the future. Wisdom comes to us in moments of still, heavenly quietness amid the wild cacophony of human noise. It begins in a place where we look up and see that God is magnificent and breathtaking and vast, sovereign and dazzlingly sufficient. Wisdom begins with the fear of the Lord. It is cultivated out of awe and reverence for his holy name, out of worship of the One who is God alone. With true wisdom we dare not second-guess God.

God chooses the 'weak and foolish' things

This is what Saul himself later wrote to the church in Corinth: 'God chooses the weak things and the foolish things in this world to confound the strong and wise.'

Why?

Because in this, God was glorified in a way that he would not be if our most likely candidate had been selected to be the apostle to the Gentiles. In every place that Saul would eventually go, in every sermon that he preached, in every soul that he led to Christ, every church that he planted and every letter that he wrote, God was glorified as the One who made Saul what he became. He acknowledges it himself when he writes about his ministry. In 1 Corinthians 2:1–5 he wrote

> When I came to you, brothers, I did not come with eloquence or superior wisdom as I proclaimed to you the testimony about God. For I resolved to know nothing while I was with you except Jesus Christ and him crucified. I came to you in weakness and fear, and with much trembling. My message and my preaching were not with wise and persuasive words, but with a demonstration of the Spirit's power, so that your faith might not rest on men's wisdom, but on God's power.

In 2 Corinthians 4, writing about way in which the light of the glory of God in Christ shines in his heart, he says 'But we have this treasure in jars of clay to show that this all-surpassing power is from God and not from us' (2 Cor. 4:7).

All the glory for what we read in Acts 9:1–19 goes to God because without God, Paul the apostle to the Gentiles would just have been Saul of Tarsus, forgotten now.

Which is interesting, isn't it? As God in his glorious strength does his work, we in our weakness leave behind a legacy that lasts for eternity. As God glorifies himself, he also ennobles us.

3

If not now, when?

Much of the writing that has come out of the Holocaust is breathtakingly beautiful. Some of it flowed from the profoundly humane and tragically injured soul of Jewish chemist, Primo Levi. He wrote, among other things, a devastating, deeply moving book about the state of humanity in the concentration camps of Nazi Germany, entitled *If Not Now, When?*[3] Levi confronts the reader with a question: if a person will not be compassionate, truthful and loyal now, when will they be such? And he confronts us with a cry: do that which is right and do it now; neither settle for the bystander's apathy nor back down in the face of overwhelming odds.

God's time for Saul to build is now.

This is the fellow-builder's question: what are you waiting for? Are you waiting for fairer weather, for more favourable conditions than presently prevail, before you will commit your life to building with God?

What particular set of circumstances are going to make you go and ask Bob about his wife's cancer, and show some of the understanding and compassion that flow from the Jesus Christ, the King of love? What has to change before you'll actually give Brenda a Bible, like the one you keep saying you've found so helpful? How many more months of chatting about important issues in life have to go by before you'll invite your neighbour Brian to the evangelistic course? Will it really have to be next year before you give your time once and for all to the prayer meeting instead of going along occasionally, on the back of decreasingly frequent bouts of guilt?

If the moments to speak, to hug, to give, to pray have been hanging on the branches of your friendships and acquaintances for long enough, don't keep waiting. You've seen them, like fruit ripe for picking. You've felt the nudge to reach out and grasp the moment but you've hesitated and in your heart you've pulled back, afraid that Brenda or Bob or Brian might say 'No'. And the moment has passed. Take heart. Don't let these moments rot on the branch.

If not now, when?

God's pace

You'll need to read Acts 9:19–31.

God moves at his own pace. We are accustomed to thinking that God is going to take a lot longer than we are. So, for instance, the advice often given to new ministers as they begin their work is to avoid rushing headlong into changing the life of the congregation, but to be patient. 'Don't change a thing for a whole year. Slowly does it.'

Unfortunately, most congregations have been waiting and searching for a new leader for some considerable time. They are desperate for somebody to come in, roll up their sleeves, and start working straight away. Most people who care don't want somebody who is going to make every effort to become part of the furniture. A 'breath of fresh air' is usually more welcome.

When you start a new job, the temptation is to ease in, let everyone get to know what your taste in coffee and music are, what football team you support, what school your kids go to and where you like to go on holiday. The plan is that when you've blended in and established that you're a normal human being and not a religious weirdo, you'll start to mention Jesus. That usually happens about three hundred years after you've plucked up courage to mention that you went to church over the weekend, which itself only happens after you got challenged by the Pastor. But God, who is better to listen to than our fears, might want you to let people know the most important thing about you first. Not in a way that makes people cringe, nor in a way that does violence to your true personality. But in a way that lodges something about following Jesus in people's perceptions of you when you talk about the football or the merits of Arabica beans.

The fact is that God can move like lightning. In the growth of the Kingdom of God, it is us who have to catch up with him. We are usually unaware of what he is doing in people's lives, of how the ground has been prepared for the word of God. We regularly miss the opportunities that exist around us for his Kingship to be extended. We need to be brought up to speed.

God moved very quickly with Saul. In the moment when God saved him, he instantly flipped the whole man, training, knowledge, motives, temperament, the right way up. According to what he wrote in Galatians 1:13ff, he would spend time away from the crowds re-working his understandings of the Hebrew Scriptures – our Old Testament – but in Acts Luke is concerned with the speed with which events unfolded: Saul was immediately enabled to proclaim the Name of Jesus the Christ, rather than work for the destruction of that Name. Filled with the Spirit at Ananias' visit, Saul was instantly empowered for service. So we read these astonishing two words in verse 20: 'at once'. At once he began to preach in the synagogues. Yes, God's pace sometimes seems slow. But God can also work with breathtaking speed. Saul's moment to serve would not be at some indefinable time called 'later'; he could not put off being God's fellow-builder until he felt more qualified or affirmed or comfortable. It was now.

Saul the Pharisee becomes Paul the preacher

Where Paul preaches

He begins a preaching tour round the synagogues of Damascus. (Note the plural in verse 21. You needed a minimum of forty Jewish males to establish a synagogue: the city was not short of Jewish men.)

What is the significance? The synagogues are the key, strategic place to preach about the Messiah. In the synagogues the scrolls of the Scriptures are available. The expectation is that, at every gathering, they will opened, read out loud and commented on. There Paul finds both Jews and 'God-fearers' – Gentiles who recognise something so compelling about Jehovah that they revere him and something so admirable in Jewish morality that they want to learn it.

Paul can reach two kinds of people and can use the accepted Scriptures to make the case for Jesus of

Nazareth being the Christ. But there is an irony to this, of course. It is in the synagogues that Saul would also encounter the Scribes and the Pharisees, for the synagogue is local HQ for the Thought Police, Command Centre for the Truth Regime. So those by whom he had been commissioned to wipe out the church now heard Saul preach the very name that they wanted to delete from history.

This is one of the most wonderful turn-arounds that God does in the book of Acts. Our God is a transforming God. Who are you praying for? What situations that seem hopeless do you keep bringing to God? You can find confidence to keep asking God for a transformation. But the confidence can't be found in your ability to pray well enough or envisage clearly enough or feel assured enough. Nor is it found in your estimate of how likely it is that Dorothy will actually ask you about Jesus, or of how capable Taz is of staying off the beer and actually studying for at least some of his time at university or that Fran will want not to go to bed with her non-Christian boyfriend. The confidence to pray about humanly unchangeable situations is in God, who has done the impossible transformation with every single one of his fellow-builders, including you. You are evidence of the power of God to save and to keep. You are the reason to be confident in God.

So God takes (of all the people on the planet) the Pharisee formerly known as Saul, into (of all places) the synagogue, where he begins to preach in (of all names) the name of Jesus to (of all groups) his former masters and accomplices.

And you worry that Dorothy's going to be too tough a case for God?

What Paul preaches

'At once he began to preach in the synagogues that Jesus is the Son of God . . . and baffled the Jews living in Damascus by proving that Jesus is the Christ' (verses 20, 22).

What was it that Paul had found most repulsive about Christians? It wasn't their style, it wasn't their clothes, their flesh-crawlingly insipid songs, their sickening nice-ness or anything like that. It wasn't what it suits the world to caricature Christians as being. What he found most disgusting was what most of the other Jewish lead-ers had found most offensive about Jesus: he claimed to be God. Remember that they nailed Jesus, literally, on a blasphemy charge. It wasn't primarily his popularity; it was that they believed he was being blasphemous. Only days previously, Paul was of the same mind; he wanted to wipe out the church because the church proclaimed the hideous blasphemy that Jesus was the Messiah. Yet by God's work within him, this man now preaches and debates and argues, amassing a bewildering array of Old Testament Scriptures, to prove that Jesus and his fol-lowers have been right all along. Jesus really is God and he really is the Anointed One, the King of the Jews. God has taken those lips which only days ago had uttered vile blasphemy against the Lord's Christ, and is now using them to prove to sceptical Jews that they, not Jesus, are the blasphemers.

And there's more. It's not simply that new interpreta-tions of the Old Testament, new doctrines, new 'takes' on old passages, are coming out of Paul's lips. It is that those lips that had once dishonoured Christ personally

now honour and glorify him. Paul preaches that Jesus is
the Son of God and proves from the Scriptures that he is
the Messiah and, by that very process, with every word
and thought, Jesus is being glorified on earth and in
heaven. Once he wanted to destroy the church of Jesus
Christ and wipe out the name of Jesus. Now Paul exalts
the name of Jesus. It's wonderful. If we can't believe God
to do saving work in our neighbourhood or among our
friends, then we might as well stay at home and clean
under the fridge. Look at what he's done here! And this
God is our God who, as Jesus said in John 5:17, is always
doing his work – this work.

How Paul preaches

He preaches with increasing power, as we read in verse
22. We read in verse 27, by which time he's back in
Jerusalem and Barnabas is speaking for him, that he
'preached fearlessly'. In verse 28 when he's actually
preaching in Jerusalem, he speaks boldly 'in the name of
the Lord Jesus Christ'. It's that word 'boldly' that gives
us the best handle on how Paul preaches. The words
bold, boldness or boldly crop up seventeen times in the
New Testament. Only once, in 2 Peter 2, is it used in a
negative sense, which there means 'impudent'. Of the
other sixteen occurrences, one is in Mark's Gospel, one is
in Luke's and the remaining fourteen either concern
Paul or are in what Paul writes. It is the byword for his
preaching and for the way in which anyone ought to
preach the gospel.

Boldness is needed today also. Not brash, abrasive
rudeness that discredits the gospel, but fearlessness;
stick-your-neck-out, take-a-risk courage. But many of us
find that worrying. Some of us are not, by temperament,
bold. We are timid. We are quiet. Does God want us to

become someone that we're not? No, but God made Paul bold with the gospel. Whenever he took hold of the sword of the Spirit which is the word of God, he was emboldened by it; as if power surged through the handle into him and made him courageous, Look at what he writes about himself to the church in Corinth: 'By the meekness and gentleness of Christ, I appeal to you – I, Paul, who am "timid" when face to face with you, but "bold" when away!' (2 Cor. 10:1). And, 'For some say, "His letters are weighty and forceful, but in person he is unimpressive and his speaking amounts to nothing"' (2 Cor. 10:10). I wonder if he warned Timothy, his son in the faith and loyal co-worker, against giving in to his natural timidity because he recognized something of himself in Timothy. 'Fan into flame the gift of God, which is in you through the laying on of my hands. For God did not give us a spirit of timidity, but a spirit of power, of love and of self-discipline. So do not be ashamed to testify about our Lord . . .' (2 Tim. 1:6–8).

This kind of boldness comes from God. We cannot stir it up in ourselves or we produce an inept and unproductive boldness that comes across as arrogance. It's certainly not something that ministers can browbeat a congregation into. We need to ask to be emboldened by the gospel so that we might be properly bold with it. As our own culture flexes its secular muscles increasingly against the church and the gospel, we need to ask God to give us courage and openness with the good news, even to our own surprise. ('Goodness! Did I really say that to Eric the supervisor, and to clever, cynical Mandy? Must have been God. So he is with me!') Boldness makes people listen who otherwise might turn an intentionally deaf

ear to the gospel. It breaks down barriers that otherwise would remain. Not least because when we are
bold, people see that what we say matters to us
enough for us to say it.

Hello suffering

Hated and shunned by the Jews

God sends Paul out as a fearless and bold preacher; he
also introduces him to suffering. The two go hand in
hand. Acts 9:23: 'After many days had gone by, the Jews
conspired to kill him.'

Recall the principle that runs through the stories of
God's fellow-builders: we, worked within, work the
works of God. Thus Saul of Tarsus, who once wanted to
wipe out the name of Jesus on behalf of the Jews, is
now being written about in ways that Luke once wrote
about Jesus: the Jews conspired to kill him. (Compare
this with Luke 19:47.) Amazingly, those who prided
themselves so much on their legalistic righteousness
according to the commandments, which say 'You shall
not kill', plotted to kill one of their own who
converted.

In the opening of his gospel, John wrote about the
same response to Jesus that now Paul, proclaiming
Jesus, experiences: Jesus came to his own people, but
they did not receive him (Jn. 1:11).

Paul's life is being re-patterned in Christ, so instead of
being a demolition expert, he becomes a builder who
works in the way the Master-Builder works. God shapes
his fellow-builders to conform to the humanity of Christ,
the perfect Servant.

Feared and shunned by the disciples

It gets worse for Paul. He is feared and shunned, initially, by the disciples in Jerusalem. Luke distinguishes between the disciples, verse 26, and the apostles that we read of in verse 27. The disciples are a larger crowd, whether Luke is referring to all the believers, or whether he means that group of about 120 or so that were there when the Spirit came down at Pentecost. So it's a large number of people that fear Paul. They don't believe he is a disciple. They can't accept that God could have turned their worst enemy into a follower of their Lord and Friend: into one of them.

Let's bring this one right home. If the drugged and drunk down-and-out, who uses your church steps as a toilet and hurls expletives at you all as you enter the building, came inside one day and said he'd become a Christian, how many folk would believe him? If your Pastor brought him in and said, 'This man has become a Christian, I've seen it happen' then maybe more of you would accept that God had done it, although I don't think everybody would.

The scepticism of the disciples is neither unusual nor incomprehensible. As Saul, he had hauled Christians out of their homes and locked them up in prison, and when the vote came to kill them, he had always voted 'Yes'. But think of it from Paul's point of view for a moment. He's become a Christian. He's started preaching the gospel. It seems reasonable to expect that some of the saints will be glad. He might have expected some suspicion, but wholesale rejection? It would have come as no surprise that the Jews turned against him: he knew exactly what they thought of Christians. But he might have expected to fare better with fellow-believers. After all, wasn't the grace of God in Christ a significant part of what they had experienced, and for which they worshipped God? And he's doing God's will, he's honouring Christ, he's doing it with boldness that comes from God. Yet nobody wants to go anywhere near him. We've seen enough in Acts already to know that being re-shaped according to Christ and working with God on the building site of his Kingdom is not a ticket to an easy life. God uses Barnabas, who vouched for the authenticity of God's work in Paul's life, to avert the loneliness of permanent double rejection: by the Jews and by the church.

A fugitive for Christ

Despite Barnabas' intervention, Paul's life takes on a quality that many in the worldwide church of Jesus Christ understand today: he becomes a fugitive. Called forward by God? Yes. Given a purpose in life that far excels his self-mapped career in professional Judaism? Yes. But the direction that the new path was to take, in day-to-day, month-to-month terms, was often illumin-ated as much by opposition, persecution and misunder-standing as by inner conviction and the voice of the Spirit. The church throughout Judea, Galilee and Samaria enjoyed a time of peace (Acts 9:31) but not until, in verses 29–30, the Grecian Jews have tried to kill him and his friends have taken him down to Caesarea and sent him off back to Tarsus. He has already had to be let down by a rope in a basket, through a window in a wall of Damascus, making an escape by night. The man who only recently had instilled fear wherever he went runs for his life.

It was going to happen all through his ministry. Paul is, in one sense, only part missionary. He is part mis-sionary and part fugitive: not at home in this world; always passing through.

What's going on? He is being taken down the road that Christ went. Luke had written Jesus' own words, 'The Son of Man has nowhere to lay his head' (Lk. 9:58). Where would Paul call home from now on? He wasn't going to go home to Tarsus and build a quiet life for himself; maybe plant a little fellowship there and settle for playing the well-respected local pastor. He certainly wasn't going to stop preaching the gospel, acknowledge the whole thing as being a great mistake and try to get back in with the Jews. He would have nowhere to call home, in the sense that he had up until he was saved. He was a fugitive for Christ.

Small wonder that later on he would write about looking ahead to heaven, about yearning to be there, about desiring to be away from the world and to be with Christ. Small wonder that he would write, 'we fix our eyes on what is unseen' (2 Cor. 4:18).

4

If not here, where? (You're already where God has put you)

The fugitive begins to experience the other side of the coin from if not now, when? That question refers to our sense of time: now is the time to be involved in building God's Kingdom. The other question has to do with where you are 'now'. It's the location thing. It follows naturally from the observations above. If not here, where? Is there some place else where we will imagine that we'll suddenly become Kingdom-builders, or will we build right here?

Places are important. The physical environment and the associations that it carries, the levels of tranquillity or stimulus, of noise and light, of warmth and space, make an impact on us that we are foolish to ignore. Some places feel like home: they 'fit' with us, our souls resonate with their surroundings. The English Lake District, bits of Yorkshire, the Cotswolds, Brittany's coast and New York do it for me. Where would you love to be? Most of us, most of the time, are somewhere else.

The point is, can your Kingdom-building thrive where you are now? Is God only really going to get the best out of you when you're 'up on the roof' or when you've got off the plane in Cambodia or in an office that's trendy, or feminine, or clean and tidy or whatever else it isn't at the moment? Is he only going to get the best from you when you're somewhere else?

Think this through with me . . .

> Now those who had been scattered by the persecution in connection with Stephen travelled as far as Phoenicia, Cyprus and Antioch, telling the message only to Jews. Some of them, however, men from Cyprus and Cyrene, went to Antioch and began to speak to Greeks also, telling them the good news about the Lord Jesus. The Lord's hand was with them, and a great number of people believed and turned to the Lord.
>
> News of this reached the ears of the church at Jerusalem, and they sent Barnabas to Antioch. When he arrived and saw the evidence of the grace of God, he was glad and encouraged them all to remain true to the Lord with all their hearts. He was a good man, full of the Holy Spirit and faith, and a great number of people were brought to the Lord.
>
> Then Barnabas went to Tarsus to look for Saul, and when he found him, he brought him to Antioch. So for a whole year Barnabas and Saul met with the church and taught great numbers of people. The disciples were called Christians first at Antioch.
>
> During this time some prophets came down from Jerusalem to Antioch. One of them, named Agabus, stood up and through the Spirit predicted that a severe famine would spread over the entire Roman world. (This happened during the reign of Claudius.) The disciples, each according to his ability, decided to provide help for the brothers living in Judea. This they did, sending their gift to the elders by Barnabas and Saul (Acts 11:19–30).

> When Barnabas and Saul had finished their mission, they returned from Jerusalem, taking with them John, also called Mark (Acts 12:25).

You'd be forgiven for thinking that this isn't one of the most earth-shattering momentous passages in Scripture. It's less dramatic than Daniel in the lions' den, less comical than Zacchaeus up the tree, and less meaty than Romans. At first glance, and even perhaps at fifth glance, it doesn't look like a particularly succulent scriptural steak into which you might sink your spiritual teeth.

Call me weird, but I think that it is foundational for the rest of Paul's story as a Kingdom-builder with God. The unfolding story of what God did in Paul, so that he shared in the building of the Kingdom and the church, is all concerned with the themes of these verses: his relationship with Barnabas and other saints, his deployment by the Spirit, his relationship with the believers in Jerusalem and the way in which the church is brought round, lock, stock and barrel, to the idea that the gospel is for the whole world, including the Gentile bits. All the building blocks are here.

God deploys people as he sees fit. Here, he begins to move around one of the most significant members of his workforce. 'You're a Roman citizen: go there. You can lift your Greek up a few notches: present the gospel over here. You can argue with Judaisers (and how!): I need you over in that corner. You've worked this Gentile thing out from the Old Testament – I want you over there to help them.' We've seen it with Philip; here, with Paul, God's doing it long-term. God makes what we might call career moves for Paul that will affect every area of his living for the rest of his days on earth.

This begins to emerge as one of the principal works of God in the lives of his fellow-builders.

God's priority in Paul's life was God's mission. That mission is to redeem 'a people' for himself and be known as God by all. Put another way, the mission is to increase the government of his Son Jesus Christ. Thus the church grows to the greater and greater glory of God This doesn't happen in Acts by congregations becoming established and then simply sitting on their seats and effectively saying, 'Well, that's neat – we're sorted, apart from few in-house issues with which we can occupy ourselves in a godly-ish manner for the rest of our lives; we'll just serve ourselves, thank you.' All those purposes of God which start in Genesis and reach their fulfilment in Revelation are accomplished through mission: God's mission, in which we participate for the whole of our lives on earth. God's priority is always mission; Acts is simply a one time-specific window on what he's doing the rest of the time. If Paul is to become a fellow-builder with God, who is on a mission, it's not exactly rocket science to see how Paul's priority has to become mission. Paul's life has to be plugged into the mission of God.

Guess who else that applies to. It's why you are still alive on earth.

You've work to do, people to see, places to visit. The first word in the vocabulary of God's mission is 'Go.'

So now this Kingdom-building stuff could become challenging. We could risk losing people from our fellowships because God wants to build his Kingdom and that's not quite the same as keeping our fellowships in the manner to which we've become addicted. Maybe we're the ones who have to be sent.

Our churches are transformed when we learn Kingdom attitudes and Kingdom-oriented decision-guiding reflexes. They stagnate and die when they subordinate the needs of the gospel to the preservation of their traditional practices. Think 'Kingdom' not 'congregation'. Individually, we need the same Kingdom-mindedness. Take the principle into the context of our jobs – what we apply for, what we're like when we're at work, how we conduct our meetings, chat over coffee, e-mail round the office, etc. Take Kingdom-mindedness to the estate agent's office and apply it to where we choose to live, or to the bank, or the hotel on a business trip. The simple but eminently missable feature of God's work in his fellow-builders in Acts is that he keeps adjusting them until their lives are plugged into his priority.

God's priority is mission. If we've got any other priority ahead of that one, we're missing the point.

Observe the details of how God connects his people with his purposes.

No mean city

After Rome and Alexandria, Antioch was the third largest city in the first century Roman Empire. Its population of half a million was a cultural melting-pot: five main people-groups – Greeks, Romans, Jews, Arabs, Persians; many more languages; even more gods. But the one true God had already moved his builders in. People had come especially from Cyprus (the home of Barnabas) and Cyrene to preach the gospel. Saints who had been scattered from Jerusalem preached as they settled there. Antioch became a focal point in God's strategy for the bold proclamation of the gospel. The church flourished among Gentiles.

The response of the Jerusalem leaders

News of this reached the ears of the church at Jerusalem (verse 22). Even the way Luke writes it makes you think, 'Here we go: the chiefs in Jerusalem will want to get their paws on it.' Without doubt, the apostles in Jerusalem wanted to exercise a degree of control or assessment, at the very least. This was no bad thing. The desire reflected a concern that the name of Jesus was not being attached to that which was nothing to do with him. Lifestyles should be holy; heresies and other distortions of the gospel should be exposed; the vulnerable should be cared for; resources should be shared. Out of the best of concerns, the church in Jerusalem wanted to know that what was going on in Antioch really was a work of grace that was led by the Spirit and not something else.

Yet it's not unlikely, given the difficulty that would emerge in chapter 15, that the apostles in Jerusalem also found the idea that the grace and the Spirit of God would be poured out on the Gentiles almost unbelievable. As well as the laudable zeal for the integrity of the gospel, there is more than a hint of suspicion that Jehovah wouldn't do something so . . . well, frankly, so un-Jewish.

The church in Jerusalem had to learn that it was not in control of the Kingdom. It also had to let go of the notion of being at the centre of everyone's relationship with God. Their responsibility, as we've seen already with the emerging pattern of God's work in his people, was to catch up with God and not to hold God in.

Put the right man in the right place at the right time

Who better to send three hundred miles north to Antioch but Barnabas? Rewind to when Barnabas first appears in Luke's unfolding story: Acts 4:36. The church in Jerusalem is thriving, all the believers were one in heart and mind; they were selling their possessions, putting the money at the apostles' feet and distributing resources to anyone as they had need. We read: 'Joseph, a Levite from Cyprus, whom the apostles called Barnabas . . . sold a field he owned and brought the money and put it at the apostles' feet.' He's from good Jewish stock, the Levitical, priestly tribe, which establishes his credibility, yet he's clearly committed to the fellowship of Christ's people.

By chapter 11 he has obviously become a respected part of the church in Jerusalem. His nickname marks out his character – 'son of encouragement': the kind of man you'd be thankful to have with you in a crisis. Luke reserves one of his rare character assessments for him, describing him as 'a good man, full of the Holy Spirit and faith', a similar phrase to that which he used to describe Stephen. His opinion is heeded in Jerusalem. His gracious courage and wisdom have already been significantly used in the progress of the church's life when Paul was shunned in Jerusalem. Barnabas had the wit to recognise that a crucial moment had arisen and the right response to God was vital. If the church in Jerusalem had not accepted that what had happened in Damascus through Paul was of God, what would that have done to their participation in the mission of God?

It's another turning point. As he travels to Antioch, once again Barnabas will be a key player in God's mission. Imagine if Barnabas had arrived with a suspicious and control-minded attitude, which is probably what some of the legalistic brothers in Jerusalem would have wanted? What if he had a fixed grid in his mind, dictating to his eyes, ears and soul that God can only work through people ABC in place PQR in an XYZ fashion? What could he not have thought? What would he have not seen and heard? What could he not discern? It would have been an absolute disaster. Imagine if verse 23 read something like, 'Yea, and when he arrived he bothered not with all that careful listening nonsense, but rather he mightily smote the false saints of Antioch and told them that verily they had better hot-foot it unto Jerusalem to be vetted by those who knowest what they talk about.'

How much of the history of churches has been skewed by precisely a fixed grid constructed out of the traditions of this or that group, which renders people blind to the work of God? You can find such grids at either end of just about any spectrum you choose: from those who believe that the gifts of the Spirit can be categorised as natural and supernatural and that the latter type ceased with the apostles, through to those who insist on the practice of every kind of gift, from tongues to tray-bakes. From those who prefer their worship aged to maturity for no less than 250 years, to those whose taste in songs is totally confined to that which has been published in this calendar year. From those who insist that if it's not led by a person in clerical garb it's not worship, to those who insist that if it's led by a human being, it's not worship. The frightening thing is that we construct such rigid grids so quickly and that we pride ourselves on the level of discernment that they give us.

Barnabas arrives in Antioch with a mind that is quick to recognise the grace of God being poured out by the Spirit of God. There's a characteristic you'd want in leadership: not command-and-control blinkered narrowness but alertness to God's grace and power.

Why is Barnabas capable of this? It's in Doctor Luke's diagnosis of his character: he is a good man who is full of the Holy Spirit. He's not full of himself or of church power or politics. He's not full of that rank, carnal approach to Christianity. He's full of the Spirit. That's what makes him quick to see the evidence of God's grace.

So instead of discouraging them, he is glad in his own heart. It's interesting that Luke takes note of what's going on inside Barnabas. The work in Antioch puts a smile on his face; he is thrilled at the situation and he encourages them all to remain true to the Lord with all their hearts. The fellow-builder builds up other believers.

Nice.

It could have gone so horribly wrong. But God had the right man in the right place at the right time.

Get the other right man

Barnabas then does the most significant thing in the passage. He goes to get the other right man. He knows that he is not the only one needed for the building of the Kingdom. All these people coming into the church need to be taught, yet there is still preaching to be done. As well as the heralding of the message of the gospel, there is also an urgent and profound need for passing on the truth received from God, the content of what we believe, to believers. This is a big city; many are becoming Christians; there's no hint that these folk from Cyprus and Cyrene should be silenced now that Barnabas is there. The proclamation continues; the church grows numerically. So now there's a growing need for a teaching ministry: in fact there is more than one man can do. Not wanting to become the apostolic bottleneck, Barnabas knows that he has to work with someone. And he knows exactly who that person is. It's Paul.

So Barnabas travels further north and then west to Paul's home town, Tarsus. He searches him out and takes him back to Antioch. Then, for a whole year, Barnabas and Paul met with the church and taught great numbers of people.

Why did Barnabas know to get Paul? Paul had already demonstrated his boldness as a preacher of the gospel in Damascus and Jerusalem; but Barnabas has discerned more than boldness. Has he seen Paul's understanding of the Old Testament or his understanding of what Christ has done in his life; was it a special gift for communicating? Whatever it was, Barnabas realises that Paul is the one to share the teaching of the new Christians in Antioch.

Think of it for a moment. Paul is as trans-cultural (able to cross cultures) as Antioch is multi-cultural. Paul, a Roman citizen trained in Greek philosophy and a Hebrew of the Hebrews, can move easily among these people. He is also free to be mobile, not least because he's single. But there's another reason why he goes for Paul. Barnabas knows, from first-hand experience, that Paul is plugged into God's priority. As far as Paul is concerned, if the sun rises in the east it's going to be a day for mission. Though he was once totally at odds with God's purposes, he is now, by the amazing conversion that we saw earlier, fully alive to them.

In *Six Habits of Highly Connected People*, Gerard Kelly writes:

Connected lives are infused with the fire of God. Connected people make a difference to their environment because they are a point of entry for grace. The choices they make, the directions they choose, the relationships they make and maintain, all these are shaped and defined by their core connection to God's purposes . . . No habit is higher and no aim more admirable than the quest to connect with God's mission. The greatest missionary endeavours in the world will count for nothing if they don't connect with the mission of God. The smallest acts of kindness are magnified beyond measure when they do. The most powerful passion will prove destructive unless it is connected to God's passion. The highest purpose will not produce life unless it is connected to God's purposes. Unconnected millions can be given and spent to no avail; connected, the widow's merest mite can touch heaven and change the earth.[4]

Two connected men serve God together on his building site; God's power is at work through their teaching; the church grows.

It's not simply a numbers game; we see the character of the church growing. Significantly, the church in Antioch becomes as responsive as their teachers, God's lightning conductors who bring his power to change their lives. The believers collect money for the troubled and impoverished church in Judea. Who better to take it there (and keep on preaching as they go) but Paul and Barnabas? But even more significantly, they become as responsive as Christ; the Missionary sent from heaven to earth, who came to do all the Father's will and only the Father's will. The great, compelling reason for the Christians in Antioch to become engaged in the mission of God is not what's going on in Paul's and Barnabas' lives so much as what went on in Jesus' life, which is being re-worked in Paul and Barnabas.

What's the implication of all this?

It is that God has us where he wants us now, so that we might be connected with his purposes for the people around us now. We can so easily think, 'I'll be more use if I was somewhere else.' Or 'I'd be more useful if I was *someone* else.' But God has us here and now because he wants us here and now, to use us here and now with our families, with our friends, with our neighbours, with our colleagues. The crucial question is: Am I connected to God's Kingdom-building purpose?

5

5

Changing the world: Paul's first missionary journey

The most unpredictable recruitment and selection process has engaged the most unlikely person on earth to share with God in the most important work in the entire world. An enemy has become a servant, a killer has become a saint. A mind that thought the truth to be a lie has been turned the right way out. A heart full of hatred has been flooded to overflowing with God's love.

Infinitely more than the average church search committee or bishop could ever have dreamed of, let alone achieved, has been accomplished by God, the Maker, Redeemer and King; in less time than it takes to write a book about it.

But what's the task? What's his job description? And what pattern of work will be set for him?

What was Paul's task?

The task can be stated simply: to change the world.

That's the commission of Jesus and it's been the work of God since Adam and Eve first fell. A changed world is the promised result of the life and spiritual warfare of the church at the end of time.

It's simple to state the task but not so simple to do. The world is big, and the world is, in terms of its attitude to God, bad: hostile to the gospel. The devil has much to lose and is hostile to God. And our flesh is so prone to yielding when tempted, so deeply enmeshed in sinful ways, so busy with serving the wrong gods.

There's so much to change within each of God's Kingdom-builders, and Paul was no exception. So now that he's got the job, or rather, now that the job's got him, what sort of on-the-job training is he going to get? What work was God going to do within Paul?

What we look at in this chapter is the way in which God carved life-long patterns of service into Paul's mind and heart. The first missionary journey, as it's usually called, wasn't just an end in itself. It had a lasting effect on Paul. What he learned as he journeyed with companions, with the gospel and with God, was to shape all his days. The imprint of it can still be seen at the very end of the book of Acts.

What God had to do in his life might not be exactly the same as he has to do in your life. But God will make the same sort of changes, speak slight variations of the same call, redirect our time and gifts into the same pattern of life that we see Paul's being directed into. It's unlikely that God will call you to serve him on an island in the Mediterranean. (It does happen though, so it might be worth praying about just in case the Lord is mulling it over.) But in other ways he will call you to 'Go' and introduce people to the one and only Saviour.

In one sense, God was simply leading Paul further along a straight line that began almost immediately after his conversion. His life as a Christian had been leading up to this: he was to spend his days 'going away'.

In the good old days, photos were developed in red-lit darkrooms. This life is a darkroom. Heaven is the gallery. Follow the metaphor with me. Three shallow trays of liquid were laid out next to the enlarger on the bench. Photo paper was exposed to the image from the negative for an accurately timed few seconds of bright white light. (More frequently, in my experience, the seconds were guessed by the secret dark-room arts.) Then the paper was carefully slid into the first tray of developer until, magically, the positive image appeared. But it could all go horribly wrong unless the paper was gently lifted out of the developer and laid in the second tray, the fixative. There, it soaked for a short time until the image was set on the paper, and thence the print went into the third tray for rinsing.

The bright, white light shone on Paul's life on the road to Damascus. Then a new life was developed; a new image emerged from the exposed paper of his life in Damascus, Jerusalem and Antioch – the first tray in the darkroom. Think of Paul's first missionary journey as the second tray, the fixative.

So far he has been travelling for the sake of the Name of the Lord Jesus Christ; part fugitive, part emissary. He would spend the rest of his life in a steady but world-changing pattern of going from a place where his work was done to a place where it had yet to start or where it needed to be nurtured. He would continue to demonstrate remarkable flexibility and creativity. He would courageously face peril, persecution and pain as he carried on working with fellow-builders at the prompting of the Spirit. In these two chapters of Acts, 13 and 14, the globally significant CV of Paul the missionary to the Gentiles begins to be written.

That steady pattern is not simply a matter of making journeys. What actually happened on that first journey becomes the norm for Paul. Viewing the history of the Western world – and eventually we will be able to view all history and see this – it's not at all too strong to say that Paul's life from here on in is concerned with God changing the world at two levels. It involves changing the world in the sense that people are taken out of the 'kingdom of this world'. The process is described in Colossians 1:13: 'For he has rescued us from the dominion of darkness and brought us into the Kingdom of the Son he loves.' All Paul's life as a journeyman preacher and teacher will conform to the needs of God's mission to change – to rescue, to save – the world through Christ, who himself saw it as a main part of his reason for living, dying and living again: 'For God did not send his Son into the world to condemn the world, but to save the world through him' (Jn. 3:17).

But there is a second dimension to the change: the course of the world is changed by what happens on this first missionary journey. The path of history, of social, religious, economic, industrial and intellectual activity, is turned by what happens on this first missionary journey. All over the world today, events, movements, trends, practices and traditions can be traced back to what happened on Paul's journey.

How did Paul go about his task?

A friend and I were driving to his offices for me to meet the staff and have a look round. On the dashboard of his car was an A6 sheet of paper. Places, times and people's names were printed in small but clear type. There were a few similar sheets around various parts of the front of the car. As we drove past fields and farms north of Inverness in the Scottish highlands, I asked him about them. He explained that they were given to him by his secretary, who knew that one small sheet of accurate information would keep him right over the next week and the next few thousand miles. The one that had first caught my eye was a summary of his itinerary for a forthcoming business trip to Germany. While away, my friend would send a steady stream of e-mails back to base, reporting what had happened in the various cities on the trip: whom he'd seen, what the outcome of the meetings had been, fresh contacts that extended the network of his business and the like.

The little sheet of paper for Paul and Barnabas would have lacked times, and instead of some place names it would probably have had a brief note saying 'Follow Spirit.' But before we read the e-mails back to base that Luke wrote for us, we can be helped by an overview of where they went on this builders' journey, and why.

A summary of the itinerary

Once Barnabas and Saul have completed their mercy-mission to Judea, they return to Antioch. It is the church there, prompted by the Holy Spirit, that sends them on this first voyage of mission from the nearby port of Seleucia.

First, they go to Salamis, on the south-eastern shore of Cyprus. (It was the obvious port to head for if you're working your way by sea and land westward from Antioch.) Travelling first to Cyprus has the added advantage of placing Barnabas on familiar territory, and there were already Christians on the island. Barnabas' nephew John Mark, along with others, joins them. From there, they make their way west to what was then the capital of the island, Paphos, and preach there; they encounter Elymas the sorcerer; they counteract the influence of the mythical goddess of love, sex and beauty, Aphrodite (after whose son the city was named) and they see the Roman Proconsul become a Christian. Saul begins to use his Roman name, Paul. Then they make another sea journey to the impressive city of Perga, where John Mark leaves them for reasons that Luke doesn't record, and from there it's due north to the other Antioch, in the region called Pisidia. Working their way east, they evangelise Iconium, Lystra and Derbe, and then they do the sensible thing and retrace their steps, revisiting the newly planted churches. This time they stay at Attalia, near Perga, and then sail back to Antioch.

The journey, made in AD 48 and 49, didn't take them very far west: they covered only two cities in Cyprus and a relatively small part of modern Turkey. But it did take them into cosmopolitan territory with a large Gentile population.

The thinking

Every itinerary has a rationale. If we were to plot on the map all the major centres of population in the area, then we would be plotting precisely the places that Paul and Barnabas visited. They preached in the big, strategic places; as people came into these larger centres for trade and commerce and to join the major routes to other regions, the gospel would spread. Of course it also meant that they could move quickly because the main routes were better and safer. Despite the *pax romana* that certainly enabled the evangelists to travel easily, nowhere was entirely free of robbers and thieves. Notice the strategy: doing it this way they could cover more miles, do more missions in more large towns and cities and influence more rural regions with the gospel. Do you catch a sense of urgency with which they build?

There's another point to the strategy. It's very clear from the earliest work of Kingdom-building in Acts that God writes his own rule-book. Its equally clear from the stories of Peter and Philip that God uses those who are quick to respond to the Spirit's prompts to go hither and thither as he builds his Kingdom. We've seen already in Paul's story that we can't second-guess God. All these things might lead us to think that we ought not to plan too much, that we shouldn't work out a sensible strategy; instead you just put your brain in neutral and wait for mystical steering by a celestial Auto-pilot. But these fellow-builders did employ a strategy. Here's a little snippet from a very readable book on global Christianity by Tim Jeffrey with Steve Chalke, *Connect!*

> Some people get put off at the thought of developing a strategy. It sounds too business-like and organised and leaves no space for spontaneity in the organic development of letting things move . . . In fact, developing a strategy is all about being deliberate, about achieving something. It makes us focus, first on what it is we want to achieve, helping to prevent us from simply going round in circles and never being effective in our efforts. Our strategy then helps us set a course to get from where we are to where we want to be. It need not be a rigid thing that acts like a straight-jacket but can allow us to evaluate opportunities that come up to see if they are actually going to get us closer to where we want to be.[5]

That's exactly what Paul and Barnabas were doing. They were working to a strategy. They were deliberate about wanting to achieve as wide a spread of the gospel as possible in a short period of time. They had clearly worked out what the best way to do that would be, and they stuck to a plan. That helped them set their course:

for instance, when they sailed from Seleucia straight for Salamis and then headed for Paphos and round to Perga. Go to the major settlements: the bigger they are, the longer we'll stay.

So the strategy helps the building work progress. Within a relatively short time, they transform the situation in the eastern Mediterranean from 'gospel going nowhere' to 'gospel going to significant places' and then to 'gospel spreading out from them all over the place'. The strategy helps them to evaluate the kind of things that they should be doing so that, for instance, when hostility breaks out in one place they go forward to the next unevangelised place and not back to a previous safe place. Barnabas and Paul employ a clear, but not inflexible, strategy.

We have a gospel to take to this world: to take to our neighbourhoods, friends, colleagues, and other people that we don't even know yet. We have a gospel that is to go over the whole earth. So we don't just sit here and expect that somehow the Spirit will waft the gospel out without us ever doing any thinking about it. We don't sit passively and expect the Spirit to waft everybody else in either. Like Paul and Barnabas, we are fellow-builders whose brains and savvy have been given to us by the One who wants to use them to his glory. He is not glorified in us if we neglect our abilities to work out what to do. We might not think that we've got much wisdom; we might be right. But God promises to give wisdom when we ask with faith. 'If any of you lacks wisdom, he should ask God, who gives generously to all without finding fault, and it will be given to him' (Jas. 1:5). There's no conflict in the text of Acts 13 and 14 between being sent by the Spirit (13:4) and employing a clearly thought-out strategy (13:5ff).

How could the life of our fellowships be changed by thinking wisely and creatively of ways to take part in the mission of God to the people he's placed us among? If we are compelled by the love of God to get to B and we are currently at A, we have to work out a route. We should always be able to adapt as the Spirit changes our plans, but reading of God's ways in Acts 13 and 14, strategic thinking is well-used when it is employed in the building of God's Kingdom.

What was God doing?

1. Guiding by the Spirit through the church

The believers in Antioch

> In the church at Antioch there were prophets and teachers: Barnabas, Simeon called Niger, Lucius of Cyrene, Manaen (who had been brought up with Herod the tetrarch) and Saul. While they were worshipping the Lord and fasting, the Holy Spirit said, 'Set apart for me Barnabas and Saul for the work to which I have called them.' So after they had fasted and prayed, they placed their hands on them and sent them off (Acts 13:1–3).

The church is waiting upon God, worshipping and fasting as they seek his guidance. Missing meals was a regular part of religious life for Jews. The point was that you set aside the eating time to spend that time in prayer because there was a particular need. It was a way of showing God that you meant business, setting normal life aside and focusing all your attention upon God. In that condition, the Christians in Antioch are in exactly the sort of position where you might expect the Spirit to say, 'Now I want you to do this.' Why? Because God had their full attention.

At how many points in a day, or how many times when we gather together as a fellowship, does God have our full attention? Do we not often have other things on our minds? If a little video screen showed everybody what we were thinking about, what would the screen show?

Since God had their full attention, they were quite likely to be able to hear his voice when he spoke. They had shut out other voices, the normal noise of a day's business. Putting everything else to one side and disciplining the body made them hungry for God and ready for the Spirit's command. It came. 'Send Barnabas and Saul': as blunt and as simple as that. We don't need to know whether it was audible or inaudible, whether it came through one person or whether everybody else had the same idea at the same time, or whether a flock of geese made the letters in the sky or whether a passing mule clip-clopped the message in Morse code. Whatever happened was so obviously of the Spirit that Luke had to write in 13:2, 'The Holy Spirit said . . .'

Notice that they carried on praying and fasting. Maybe they wanted to check it out. Maybe they knew it was an enormous thing that they were being called to, maybe they wanted to spend more time close to God like this, enjoying and praising him for answered prayer. They didn't suddenly get on their horses and ride off in all directions. They kept giving God their whole attention for a while, lingering in the consciousness of the presence of God.

Then, without the need for anything else worth mentioning, they placed their hands on Paul and Barnabas and sent them off.

Being guided by the Spirit, through the church, is part of the pattern that is being laid down in Paul's life. On all his missionary journeys Paul never acts like some loose cannon going off on his own, as if he has his own personal hotline that everybody else has to ignore. There are times when God very clearly speaks to Paul to guide him. But in the great endeavours of his missionary journeys he acts simply as one of the church sent by the others and by the Spirit. So Paul and Barnabas are sent and authorised by the Holy Spirit through the church.

What else is God doing?

2. Commanding costly and consistent obedience

When you drive a car in a straight line, your hands are constantly moving the steering wheel. If you weren't making these little changes in direction, you wouldn't keep to the line. Weird, but true. If you don't believe me, try it – perhaps on an old aerodrome, certainly well away from other traffic.

The journey involves many adjustments to the directions that Paul and his companions take. Yet God is commanding costly obedience that will take them further along the same line as their Kingdom-building has already taken them. It's a 'long obedience in the same direction.' It's the same direction, because Paul and Barnabas have already travelled and preached the gospel as they went.

The journey will take these Kingdom-builders into new territory – new for them and for the gospel. Yet all that

Paul will encounter is the kind of thing that he's encountered from the day he was converted. Recall his progress so far. He began preaching in Damascus. He excited hostility and had to flee. He went down to Jerusalem, preached boldly there and excited more hostility. He created controversy within the church. He's been teaching for a whole year in Antioch along with Barnabas. He has a massive wealth of Old Testament knowledge in his mind readily available for arguing that Jesus is the Messiah, the Christ. New places, new people, but the same direction in which God has already been calling him.

Your circumstances might change rapidly and dramatically, or your life might seem to be an unending series of little adjustments to each day's routine. But look at your life differently: God has always wanted the same of you. The daily handling of the steering wheel might involve many adjustments, yet when you look back, can you see that in fact God has been taking you in a straight line? Even major lurches in your job, family, health or church have only served to take you further on the same line. Were you artistic when you were younger – did you always want to work with children, or live in the country, or run your own business, or preach or . . .? Is it not the case that our circumstances have had to change in order for something to emerge that has always been there?

It's costly progress though, and not just in terms of persecution. Paul's never going to retire and enjoy luxury or ease. He's never going to put his feet up and sit in his garden with nice long, cool drinks in the evening. He's never going to get to play with grandchildren. It will go on costing him all his life down here.

God will always command costly obedience in the same direction. It was the case for his Son; it will be the same for us. The choice for God's fellow-builders is to obey or not. We don't get to say, 'Well, Lord, I'm a joiner and I'm pretty good with the stonework. I can do plumbing too, and I'm not bad as an electrician. But don't ask me to do tiling and I could no more fit carpets than fly through the air. You can ask me to do the other things for you, Lord, but I'll not have you giving me the tiling job.' It is the Master-Builder who says, 'Do this, do that, go there. You've finished that job, I want you to try that one now and go to that part of the house and help the people there.' God is audacious. He is quite simply the Boss. It is the yielded and lead-able missionaries, who respond to him being the Boss, who do the building.

So what happened as they obeyed the command of God in the fellowship of the church? What does God teach them? How does he work within them so that they work the works of God?

We follow Luke's e-mailed accounts of the 'business trip', reading the memos of the meetings, the events and the progress of the work. As we read them, we'll unpack them.

6

E-mailed memos from the builder's business trip

From Paphos
**Subject: Satanic opposition – just like Jesus
endured: Acts 13:4–12**

What does God teach them about costly obedience in the
cultured and affluent capital of Cyprus? He teaches
them that wherever they go, they are going to receive
satanic opposition. Simply preaching the gospel will
excite demonic resistance.

'. . . Elymas the sorcerer (for that is what his name
means) opposed them and tried to turn the proconsul
from the faith' (13:8). The enemy launches a two-pronged
attack. He wants to dissuade the Christian from speaking
the message and at the same time he wants to harden the
heart of the non-Christian against the message.

What's the reaction of Paul and Barnabas? After
all, this is a new and unpleasant experience. They've
experienced opposition from religious people on doctrinal grounds before, but this is 'dark arts' stuff. Well,
of course they back down immediately. 'This is a bit
steep,' they say. 'Let's go back to Antioch. We can do a

cosy little teaching ministry there. Set up for life, we were, in Antioch.'

Perhaps not.

'Saul, who was also called Paul, filled with the Holy Spirit . . .' (Acts 13:9). How often we have seen that phrase as we've been going through Acts. The Spirit fills them again, recharging them for this incident, for this moment. Faster than the devil's discouragement, the Spirit comes to help them. Never suspect that you've used up all your celestial credit. God will never tire of coming to your aid.

'. . . looked straight at Elymas and said . . .'

. . . and what he said was neither winsome nor gracious. Wham! He just hits him right in the face with the truth. But do you notice he is not just speaking to Elymas? Look closely at verse 10: 'Will you never stop perverting the right ways of the Lord?'

Elymas has only just started perverting the right ways of the Lord, but Saul sees that behind him there is an opposition which has been going on for countless ages. So he parries the attack from Elymas, but he also speaks over the shoulder of Elymas to the devil behind him. ' "Now the hand of the Lord is against you. You are going to be blind, and for a time you will be unable to see the light of the sun." Immediately mist and darkness came over him, and he groped about, seeking someone to lead him by the hand' (verse 11).

As we've seen already in Acts, God always wins. He uses Paul's immediate and robust engagement in spiritual warfare and turns the hindrance to the gospel into a stepping stone to salvation for Sergius Paulus, the Roman proconsul and the most politically and socially significant man on Cyprus. The devil doesn't exactly score an own goal but he certainly does give the ball away to the church's best striker. The very thing that the devil tries to use to stop the gospel reaching the proconsul becomes the very thing that convinces the proconsul that what these men are teaching is the truth. Sergius sees the miracle and believes the message: 'When the proconsul saw what had happened, he believed, for he was amazed at the teaching about the Lord' (verse 12). Sergius is not amazed at the miracle, but at the teaching. So he doesn't say, 'Wow! That was a powerful miracle.' He says, 'The teaching must be true.' Paul and Barnabas never evangelise with signs and wonders, since they are not the good news. God might choose to show them but they only ever serve the teaching and preaching of the gospel.

As a fellow-builder, look out for satanically inspired opposition to the gospel; those who are being persuaded by the truth can be the focus of attempts to discredit Christ. Read the situation and engage, through prayer, in the spiritual warfare that rages over souls. And do so with confidence that God, who has disarmed the diabolical powers through the cross, will powerfully cause that which opposes him to serve his purposes.

From Pisidian Antioch
Subject: Bold preaching, Jewish jealousy and a revolution in world history: Acts 13:13–52

One hundred miles north of Perga, on a high plateau dotted with small lakes, stood the most important city of southern Galatia. Its population was a vibrant fusion of traditions from Greece, Rome, the Orient, Judaism and the ancient kingdom of Phrygia. Far from being daunted, Paul and Barnabas are familiar with this kind of situation.

It resembled the Antioch that they had come from, the one in the Roman province of Syria. And the gospel is not altered.

They go to the synagogue and, on the invitation of the leaders (who got more than they bargained for!) to give a word of encouragement, they preach boldly. Paul totally reworks the Judaism that was so deeply ingrained in the minds of their hearers. Skilfully, he appeals to their common ancestry and shows, from Old Testament texts that they all know but which are so tragically misunderstood, that God has always been at work through the history of his people to bring the Messiah. He hits the big themes and names of the Old Testament: Egypt; the overthrow of the lands of the seven nations when God brings them into the Promised Land; he's got Samuel in there together with Saul and David. He refers to major events where God was clearly at work, blessing his people according to his covenant and anointing kings to lead them. It's only a short step to the Anointed One, to the Messiah, to the gospel of Jesus Christ.

'Brothers, children of Abraham, and you God-fearing Gentiles, it is to us that this message of salvation has been sent. The people of Jerusalem and their rulers did not recognise Jesus, yet in condemning him they fulfilled the word of the prophets that are read every Sabbath.' And then they come to the resurrection after the crucifixion. 'We tell you the good news. What God promised our fathers . . .'

How sensibly Paul preaches! He strikes common ground as soon as possible but transforms their understanding, showing how it all leads to Jesus.

'. . . he has fulfilled for us, their children, by raising up Jesus'. Paul quotes from some of the Psalms to highlight the truth and then proclaims forgiveness of sins in verse 38: 'I want you to know that through Jesus the forgiveness of sins is proclaimed to you. Through him everyone who believes is justified from everything you could not be justified from by the Law of Moses.'

How reasonable, therefore, to sound the warning bell inherent within the gospel: Take care . . .

What a clear and compelling gospel message he gives to them. You really can't do any better, when the opportunities arrive. Search for the common ground where the common understanding is. Use that to lead people's thoughts to Jesus Christ, to the cross and the resurrection. Hold out the gospel promise of the forgiveness of sins. Warn them that their response has eternal consequences. It's not just Paul's pattern: it's the kind of thing that Jesus did throughout his ministry.

Like Jesus, Paul alters the course of world history. For here, in Pisidian Antioch, momentous words were spoken to the cynical and jealous Jewish leaders. The people wanted to hear more of the good news about Jesus after Paul had preached: they gathered in crowds to hear them again on the next Sabbath, but it was too much for the leaders of the synagogue. Made stubbornly hostile by pride and jealousy, the Jewish leaders rejected the message.

'Then Paul and Barnabas answered them boldly: "We had to speak the word of God to you first. Since you reject it and do not consider yourselves worthy of eternal life, we now turn to the Gentiles"' (verse 46). That simple phrase marks a turn in the course of history of the world. 'We now turn to the Gentiles.' The church and the world would never be the same again. That day, at that untrumpeted moment, the promise of Jehovah to his faithful servant in Isaiah 49:6 began to be fulfilled: 'It is too small a thing for you to be my servant to restore the tribes of Jacob and bring back those of Israel I have kept. I will also make you a light for the Gentiles, that you may bring my salvation to the ends of the earth' (Is. 49:6).

The Gentiles received the gospel with joy; the Jews resisted it with jealousy and drove the evangelists out of the city. Among the Jews the gospel shrivelled; through the Gentiles it spread all over the region.

In Pisidian Antioch God cast the die for the rest of Paul's ministry, and for the worldwide growth of the Kingdom. And we don't even know the date!

From Iconium
Subject: More Jewish hostility and the battle for minds: Acts 14:1–7

Luke's e-mail from what is now Konya, a Turkish city of some three-quarters of a million people, gives a brief glimpse of one of the most strategic battlelines on which the Kingdom of God opposes the kingdom of this world. It's the battle for the mind.

The opposition suddenly finds itself on the back foot. Paul and Barnabas speak 'so effectively' that many Jews and Gentiles in and around the synagogue turn from the established position that the Messiah hadn't come, to the truth that he has come and that he is called Jesus. What people think when they hear the gospel will become a frequent arena of warfare as Paul and his companions argue the case for Jesus being God and Saviour. The intellect is not spiritually neutral territory. Satan seeks to block the truth from gaining entry into the fallen human mind. He reinforces the intellectual barricades to repel the message of grace and repentance that calls everyone to follow the one true God. As it says in verse 2 of chapter 14, 'But the Jews who refused to believe stirred up the Gentiles and poisoned their minds against the brothers.'

With the mind we not only understand propositions and accept or reject them, we shape our intentions. With the mind we decide in advance that we won't listen to someone; we fix our prejudices against that which is new or that which comes from the mouths of the non-kosher. Poison the mind, and the truth or otherwise of an evangelist's words will be irrelevant. By poisoning the minds of the hearers, the words won't get through.

Back to the question that we asked very near the beginning of the book: who would you have chosen to take the gospel to the Gentiles? If we hadn't chosen Saul of Tarsus, we might well have found ourselves stuck at this point. Saul was a natural for this kind of work. He was a legal eagle, with as sharp and argumentative a mind as you could have found. Like any good barrister, he always saw the reply and was pugnacious enough to make it. God had his man in place. Paul and Barnabas do not back down, counting the battle for the mind lost before the enemy is engaged. Instead they speak 'boldly for the Lord'.

They're not just speaking to defend a cause, or to win an argument, as if the gospel were simply a set of impersonal ideas and statements. It's way more personal than that. It's good news about the One who is the most important and wonderful Person in the universe and who is also their Friend. The poison in the minds of the Gentiles concerns not simply what they think about their own state before God; it concerns the honour and reputation of the Lord. Paul and Barnabas speak boldly because they are sticking up for their Friend. Who, as it turns out, is listening. And who appears to be pleased with what he hears Paul and Barnabas doing, because he says his Almighty

'Amen' to what they have been saying and joins in the fray
with heavenly firepower. He enables them to do the kind
of messianic signs that Jesus did – miracles that fill people
with wonder and sort out who's for and who's against. It's
always useful when the infantry gets a bit of air support
from the helicopter gunships!

God also deploys the intelligence services: who and
how we'll never know, but someone eavesdrops on the
conspiracy to stone the apostles. So they leave and take
the gospel eighteen miles south-southwest to Lystra; the
refined, aristocratic, Roman colony which Timothy
probably came from, and where the greatest contests of
all would begin.

From Lystra and Derbe
Subject: The Big Issue: Who is God? ('Not us,'
say the dynamic duo): Acts 14:8–20

As Luke signs off the short memo re Iconium, he slips in
a little comment that reminds us that God uses the keen-
ness of his servants to make them flexible. They are
undoubtedly city-positive, viewing the cities as strategic
centres of influence. But these men are not used to staying quiet about their Lord, so they also take the good
news to the surrounding country. Rural Lycaonia gets
the gospel. Their city-oriented strategy was good, but
their strategy had not become their god.

Take whatever opportunities arise for Kingdom-
building; don't be so tunnel-visioned that you can't
step out of the routine. Any fellow-builder who
won't flex when the advance of the gospel is well-
served by flexibility had better check who they think
their work is serving.

It's a memo with two parts: the first concerns the humility and reverence of God's fellow-builders; the second concerns the battleground of who actually is God around here.

As they arrive in well-heeled, well-educated and highly cultural Lystra, Paul does the kind of thing that Peter had done at the Beautiful Gate in Jerusalem only a few years before. He looks directly at a crippled man and tells him to stand up on his feet ('Do the impossible!') and the man jumps up and walks. Just like that. The crowd of Lycaonian-speaking onlookers reacts by connecting miracle to deity and declaring Barnabas and Paul to be two of the biggest and best gods who ever have come down from Olympus in human form.

There's a background to Luke's memo. Lystra had two grand temples. One was to Zeus, the other was to Hermes. Zeus was the victorious and supreme ruler of Mount Olympus and of the pantheon of gods who lived there. He divided the realms among his brothers: Poseidon got the sea, Hades got the underworld. Zeus himself upheld law, justice and morals, which made him the spiritual leader of the other gods and the god in charge of civic life. Some seven centuries before Paul and Barnabas arrived in Lystra, he had been described as 'the lord of justice'. He had other titles: *Kosmetas* (the one who establishes order in the cosmos), *Soter* (the saviour), *Polieos* (the overseer of the polis, the city) and *Eleutherios* (the one who guarantees freedom). He threw bolts of lightning around, commanded the energies of the weather, sent rain, routed his many enemies and provided humankind with all that it needed for a well-ordered life. Countless festivals, including the Olympic Games, celebrated his power and goodness and he enjoyed some one hundred and fifty honourable descriptions. One form of his name is *dios*, which means 'bright', as in 'shining with brilliant splendour'. As well as carrying a bolt of lightning he was usually pictured carrying a sceptre: as far as the Greeks were concerned, he was the 'Almighty, Glorious and Venerable Ruler of Heaven and Earth'.

Ring any bells?

Zeus' son was the swift-footed Hermes (no, not the god of headscarves!) As well as being the god of a host of trades, travellers and worthy causes (and thieves and poets), he was the messenger of the gods. He carried the word from his father Zeus and spoke it to humankind. He is often pictured as wearing a winged cap and winged boots. Indeed, he is currently the emblem of the Greek Post Office. He rescued people from powerful captives: he saved Odysseus, for instance, twice; and saved his father's lover Io from the hundred-eyed giant, Argus. He was also a shepherd and the god of shepherds. He guided people as well as sheep and goats: he guided them beyond the grave to the underworld.[6]

Again, it sounds familiar, doesn't it?

Lystra revelled in these two major gods. When the cripple was healed on Paul's command, they immediately translated that which was supposed to speak of the one true and living God and of his son Jesus into the thought-world that was ruled by their great, lifeless statues.

'"The gods have come to us in human form!" Barnabas they called Zeus, and Paul they called Hermes because he was the chief speaker. The priest of Zeus, whose temple was just outside the city, brought bulls and wreaths to the city gates because he and the crowd wanted to offer sacrifices to them' (verses 11–12). If minds clashed in Iconium, gods clashed in Lystra.

Wherever the Kingdom of God penetrates the kingdom of this world, we will experience a clash of gods. Underlying the clash of world-views or values and religious traditions, there is always this titanic struggle. The question that the gospel always brings to the surface is 'Who will you have as your God?' The issue of whether people accept God as the one true God, and Jesus Christ as his Son on God's terms, or translate the truth about him into their terms, is never far from the surface. Our less classical gods give us what we want and we picture and celebrate them according to our legends (the god 'Money' is the one who gives you happiness and security. Sex, the god of pleasure, will also give you freedom. And so on.) People do exactly the same still: your God ought to give me what I want. I must be able to appease or please him with my sacrifice, and then he will do my bidding. Whatever you want to tell me about your God, it must fit my prior definition of what gods do. And I'll not see your god as a threat to mine, but simply as another version of mine.

Representing God – ironically, being heralds of the one true God – Paul and Barnabas are horrified by the irreverence shown towards God. The reaction of the people and priests in Lystra disturbs them deeply. They don't bask in the adulation for a few fleshly moments and then tell them off. They are cut to the quick that the crowd should be doing this. 'They tore their clothes and rushed out into the crowd, shouting: "Men, why are you doing this? We too are only men, human like you."' Without any advance warning, these fellow-builders are taught on the spot to be alert to the contest between gods, and to exercise total humility. Instantly they have to perceive the fundamental issue and shun all honour.

These are not easy lessons. We all prefer an easy chat about how nice God is to an all-out clash of world-views. We all like accolades and affirmation. We can dodge the basic conflicts and soak up warm praise with frightening ease. But God's fellow-builders need to develop shrewd quick-wittedness and fast-acting humility. Building the Kingdom is about God. It's not about what people think of me.

Having repelled the tribute, surely out of a reflex-like fear of the Lord rather than a sense of doctrinal appropriateness, they seize the moment both to ascribe the glory to God and to communicate the truth. Because they come from this culture, they know all that stuff about Zeus and Hermes (well, apart from the Greek Post Office bit). So they know exactly what to say. 'We are bringing you good news, telling you to turn from these worthless things to the living God, who made heaven and earth and sea and everything in them.'

Paul counters the mistranslation of events that the people had instinctively made: he points away from himself to the living God of all things and all realms. It is he who controls the weather and the crops, who provides them with all that they need to their joy, who exerts his power and goodness even for those that go their own way and do not acknowledge him. Talk about culturally apt preaching! Paul's not got to the heart of the gospel yet, to the cross, but the role of God as Maker and Sustainer of all things keeps emerging in his message as a necessary first part of the gospel. It means that we owe God because we depend upon him; that he has a claim upon us; that he loves us, for he provides for us and will call us to account.

The point of conflict became the entrance for the truth.

It might be a group of colleagues talking about work/life balance or a few fellow-students talking about debt; it might be another mum at the school gates, talking about debt and university fees or helping her teenage daughter to avoid pregnancy; it might be a pal at the clay-pigeon shoot who's sure that everything is down to chance and there's no meaning to life (particularly the way he's shooting!); whatever the point at which the worlds collide, we use that as the opening and find the way in. But we have to have an ear to hear the door creak open and we have to have the right questions to take through the door. We have to see that the next ten minutes of conversation aren't really about what they think of us but about Jesus being glorified. Most of all, we have to want to do this.

With abrupt interruption, Jews from the previous two cities arrive and sway the fickle crowd – one minute they worship Paul as the 'Messenger of the Gods' and Barnabas as the 'Supreme Ruler of all Creation'; the next minute they are stirred by the Jews into trying to kill them. Where have we seen that before, I wonder? God will lead you in the way of Christ, you know, he really will.

This time the attack comes not as a secret plot that accidentally leaks its information ahead of the attempted execution. This time it comes so fast that the stones are raining down and Paul is dragged out and left for dead before anyone can intervene.

Why no helicopter gunship this time? Perhaps there was still some gospel to be preached. Maybe the new converts (the disciples, note in verse 20) who circle him round – praying, perhaps, as well as tending his bruised and battered body – could demonstrate Christian care to the good citizens of Lystra. We don't know, but it is a beautiful picture of the care of brothers and sisters for Paul, and it certainly shows the Jews in Lystra that you really can't keep a good man down.

If we take Paul's later words to the church in Corinth into account, this kind of treatment from crowds would prepare Paul for the task of comforting and encouraging persecuted believers later in his ministry.

> Praise be to the God and Father of our Lord Jesus Christ, the Father of compassion and the God of all comfort, who comforts us in all our troubles, so that we can comfort those in any trouble with the comfort we ourselves have received from God. For just as the sufferings of Christ flow over into our lives, so also through Christ our comfort overflows. If we are distressed, it is for your comfort and salvation; if we are comforted, it is for your comfort, which produces in you patient endurance of the same sufferings we suffer (2 Cor. 1:3–6).

Many a preacher has been prepared for the pastoral element of preaching in the school of hard knocks. As Paul says to them on the return leg of the journey, 'We must go through many hardships to enter the kingdom of God' (verse 22).

'After the disciples had gathered round him, he got up and went back into the city. The next day he and Barnabas left for Derbe.' Although it was a sixty-mile hike and a roaring success, Derbe appears almost as a P.S. at the bottom of Luke's memo, so smooth, so incident-free was the entrance of the gospel into hearts in that city. Perhaps the Spirit who inspired Luke thinks that we have more to learn from the way God worked in the lives of his fellow-builders when the building was arduous than from the times when it was easy.

Derbe was the end of the line on this first journey. The evangelists lay down a pattern that will be followed later: visit, strengthen the saints and leave leaders. The leaders might have to be new Christians if they are the only ones around – it might not be ideal and certainly Paul later advises Timothy against giving new Christians leadership responsibility in case it makes them conceited (1 Tim. 3:6) – but he's prepared to 'build the walls with the bricks he's got'. So, verse 23 of chapter 14: 'Paul and Barnabas appointed elders for them in each church and, with prayer and fasting committed them to the Lord, in whom they had put their trust.'

Interesting, isn't it? How much would you trust new converts? Or more to the point, how much would you trust God in a situation where there were no long-standing converts? How peacefully could you have committed the situation to God and moved on, if you were clear that God was moving you on? The answer is an indication of how much you trust him with his church and his mission. I don't think that Luke is prescribing how to appoint leaders here; he's describing how it was done so that we can understand that God is Lord of the church and that trusting the life of the church to him is foundational to our service.

They don't stop preaching either. When they get to Perga, verse 25, and then when they go down to Attalia to catch the boat, they still preach the gospel. From Attalia they sail back to Antioch and to the church that had first sent them in the power of the Spirit, and to whom they now give a full account of the opening of the door of faith to the Gentiles.

It's a training programme

The witness expands geographically and culturally; the church grows as the word of God is taught, and opposition is stirred.

Is that all? Is God doing anything else in his co-missionaries lives? Yes. Through all these experiences he is training them for the next step, shaping his fellow-builders for bearing faithful witness in the future, when their work will be even more drastically cross-cultural. The pattern that is laid down on this first journey will be followed again on the second and third but not reproduced exactly. God's expectations are that we will proclaim his gospel and not our version of it, that we will pay a price for clashing with the world's mindset and its gods, that we will grow in our obedience to the King through hardship more than through ease. But God never expects these things to be done in unchanging circumstances nor by unchanging friends.

God is constantly creative and never repetitive. Like a Bach fugue or a well-turned phrase in a Mozart concerto, the apparent repetition is never quite that simple. There is always a variation, a fresh harmony or cadence, a development that will lead to a new phrase. We change. The church changes. The tempter tries fresh tactics. The world around us is in constant flux. So Paul's next journey, and the one after that, and the one that he will make to imprisonment in Rome and the final journey before his death will differ in much, but will all follow the broad outlines that Luke's memos suggest. And so God's house will be built; and the workers will develop.

Expect change. It's going to happen anyway, so you might as well not set yourself up for a disappointment. In fact, if you accept that there will be no end to the increase of Christ's government and peace, as God has stated in Isaiah 9:7, then you will want changes to take place because of what they produce. For God is at work in the changes, not despite them, to bring people to the acknowledgment of his Son. He is also developing your building skills and honing your resemblance to his glorious Son.

Being on this building site is an on-the-job training scheme which lasts the whole of life. We never have 'arrived' down here. We may end up changing our own building work as the years go by. Youthful vigour, coupled as it usually is with maximum free time and minimum responsibility, will give way to mid-life exhaustion and maximum responsibility (or so I'm told – by my own body!), which will in turn give way to the quieter work of old age. It is always an on-the-job training scheme for every Christian. There are always new lessons to learn in new situations. There is always fresh opposition. We are always being trained and shaped by God.

7

Ouch!
(when fallenness shows)

In all the work that we've seen so far, we've only seen 'success' – not necessarily in terms of mass repent-ances, but in terms of the faithful obedience of God's fellow-builders. By and large, that's what Acts is full of. God does his work within his fellow-builders, they respond and learn, the gospel is preached and the mis-sion of God advances through the sin-sick world that he loves.

Thus far, the companionship between Paul and Barnabas has been part of the success story. Their teamwork has not only facilitated much of the mission, it has itself been a fruit of the mission of God. Together, they have been commissioned by the council of church leaders in Jerusalem to take a letter to Antioch that will clear the way, with respect to doctrine and fellowship, for the gospel to progress into the Gentile world unfet-tered by Judaism. As Jew and Gentile are united by the grace of God in Christ, barriers of race, religion, lan-guage and culture are swept aside by the gospel.

But before this glorious spread of the Kingdom, it all takes a sudden, brief and agonising nose-dive.

Whatever we think of the issue that Paul and Barnabas fell out over just before the second missionary journey, it is a sad moment and it hurts. On one level, the lessons about the building of God's Kingdom that emerge are couched in negative terms – how not to do it. But this incident has another level of significance which I firmly believe challenges us to assess in more positive terms exactly where our confidence and hope for the building of God's Kingdom are placed. It forces us to ask ourselves whether or not we will build with God by faith in him. I believe that we are compelled by this incident to choose between despondency and poised assurance; to panic or to trust in the midst of chaos.

Before we mull over the work of God, we need to read our way attentively into the passage and take note of the details and of the vocabulary. Luke was a very careful writer.

> Some time later Paul said to Barnabas, 'Let us go back and visit the brothers in all the towns where we preached the word of the Lord and see how they are doing.' Barnabas wanted to take John, also called Mark, with them, but Paul did not think it wise to take him, because he had deserted them in Pamphylia and had not continued with them in the work. They had such a sharp disagreement that they parted company. Barnabas took Mark and sailed for Cyprus, but Paul chose Silas and left, commended by the brothers to the grace of the Lord. He went through Syria and Cilicia, strengthening the churches (Acts 15:36–41).

It's not half as calm as it reads in our English translations, neither is it as pain-free as the measured understatements suggest.

First, the word in Greek that we have as 'sharp dis-agreement' (verse 39) is much more violent; relationally if not physically. It's the word *paroxusmos*, from which we get our English word 'paroxysm'. The Greek-speaking Jews, as they produced a Greek version of the Hebrew Old Testament, used it to translate the Hebrew word *qet-seph*, which describes the fierce anger and deep indigna-tion of God. Luke describes the kind of anger that creates a violent seizure, a great heaving and wrenching apart of the relationship and of the shared carrying of the gospel.

Second, behind the rather polite and very English 'parted company' is the Greek word *apochorizo*, which means 'to sever'. Far from implying a simple, mild 'part-ing' ('Toodle-pip, old chap') the word implies a signifi-cant amount of energy and movement. The only other place that it's used in the New Testament is when the heavens flee from the presence of God on the day of his wrath in Revelation 6:14. Read the verses around it: they hardly describe a quiet afternoon's scene-shifting. The nuances of language that Luke employs here tell us that this was no amicable agreement to differ. Paul and Barnabas, of all people, suddenly tear shreds off each other verbally and then storm out of each other's com-pany, their companionship overwhelmed by wrath.

It really must have hurt the body of Christ as well as the two men. And can we imagine for a moment that Christ would not have felt it deeply?

Phew – a mistake at last! Or – hope for the human among us?

Having said that, there may be something in us that can-not help finding a slightly perverse encouragement in all this.

At the very least, it often brings consolation to find that the people in Scripture are human after all. In Luke's unfolding stories of God's work in people so that they might do his works, that's as crucial as the fact that this is a painful and terrible thing. We are looking at human beings; we're not being shown an impersonal building programme that we just scan as if we were computers and take to church-planting or personal evangelism or whatever. What would it be like if the only record we had was of great heroes of the faith who never put a foot wrong? It would paint a picture that wasn't true, but it would also be hugely discouraging.

In fact, the record is of what God has to do in their lives in order to make them fellow-builders, precisely because not one of them was by nature a fellow-builder of God's Kingdom. God had to work in them. Paul and Barnabas were as much a part of his redeeming mission as those to whom he sent them. Where would that leave us if God had to make them perfect before they would be any use? Doomed to ineffectiveness. The Scriptures are refreshingly honest: far more so than we have often been when we have written about the history of mission and crafted many a Christian biography; more honest than we often are in our fellowships.

We should, if anything, have been waiting for jagged rocks in an otherwise calm sea. The Bible itself teaches us to expect this kind of problem. The Preacher, in Ecclesiastes 7:20, says 'There is not a righteous man on earth who does what is right and never sins.' Paul himself writes

> I know that nothing good lives in me, that is, in my sinful nature. For I have the desire to do what is good, but I cannot carry it out. For what I do is not the good I want to do; no, the evil I do not want to do – this I keep on

doing. Now if I do what I do not want to do, it is no longer I who do it, but it is sin living in me that does it. So I find this law at work: When I want to do good, evil is right there with me (Rom. 7:18–21).

And James writes: 'We all stumble in many ways. If anyone is never at fault in what he says, he is a perfect man, able to keep his whole body in check' (Jas. 3:2).

Neither Paul nor Barnabas were perfect men. They were righteous men, yes; made righteous in Christ and well sanctified in many ways.

So there is hope for the human among us. We too can be used for building the Kingdom. It's no use saying, 'Oh, when I'm a better Christian I might be some use.' You can't put your own lack of sanctification up as a valid excuse for living for yourself and not for the sake of God's mission. God only ever works down here with imperfect and complicated raw material. Not one of us is pure and unalloyed. So you, like Paul and Barnabas, can be useful. You can be a fellow-builder now. We are imperfect but God is not bound by our imperfections. He is God.

What they fell out over

John Mark's reliability is the issue. John Mark (John is his Hebrew name and Marcus his Roman name) is the son of Mary who stays in Jerusalem. She isn't one of the Marys in the gospel, but another Mary, a sister of Barnabas, who therefore must also come from Cyprus. (John Mark is called a 'cousin' of Barnabas in Colossians 4:10, but the Greek word for cousin is most frequently used for a sister's son or a brother's son: that is a nephew. In fact, it is the Greek word *anepsios*, from which we get 'nepotism'; literally, favouring your nephew.) Thus, in Acts 12:12, when Peter is released from prison and it actually dawns on him that he is free, 'he went to the house of Mary the mother of John, also called Mark, where many people were gathered and were praying'. It is not unlikely that John Mark had been converted under Peter's influence, since Peter refers to him as 'my son' – that is, his son in the faith – in 1 Peter 5:13.

He had been taken by Barnabas and Paul from Jerusalem to go to Antioch when they had finished their goodwill mission to take money from Antioch to Jerusalem. 'When Barnabas and Saul had finished their mission, they returned from Jerusalem, taking with them John, also called Mark' (Acts 12:25). They then took John Mark on the first missionary journey. When they arrived at Salamis, they proclaimed the word of God in the Jewish synagogues. 'John was with them as their helper' (Acts 13:5). Keep the word 'helper' in mind.

We've seen that they went through the island of Cyprus to the western port of Paphos, from where they sailed back to the mainland at Perga in Pamphylia. But when they got there, John Mark would not go on with them. 'John left them to return to Jerusalem' (Acts 13:13).

Again, Luke's choice of words is illuminating. Behind our word 'left' is the word for abandoning or, like a soldier who has lost his nerve, deserting. It's connected to the word that described Paul and Barnabas parting company. This form of it, *apochoreo*, carries the idea of moving away from someone or a place of work with a lack of concern for what has been left. We don't know why he fell away from them, so there's no profit in speculating; but as to the tone of the departure, it was more like Paul and Barnabas' row than an affably breezy departure to catch the 6:43 up to Antioch.

Why did they fall out?

1. Different personality types

It's difficult not to see a difference of personalities here. Paul is argumentative by nature. He could argue his way out of anything, or sometimes argue his way into anything. Paul will always see the logical path to take and pursue it, despite what others might think. Once he sees where he's going to go, he's a head-down-and-off-we-go type. Barnabas, by contrast, has always been the supportive, encouraging, put-your-arm-round-some-one-and-bring-them-back-into-the-fellowship type of person. As he has been with Paul, ironically. Paul is a natural line man, Barnabas is a pure staff. Paul is the natural leader, Barnabas the natural manager who will keep everyone on board.

2. Different expectations

Their different personalities give them, in part, quite different expectations of people. Paul's natural expectation is that everybody else will follow and he would be happy if they followed at his pace as well. 'I'm going, follow me and keep up at the back there – no slacking!' Certainly at this stage in his life, we've yet to see the Paul that will write the letters, in which a more pastoral side will emerge. He sets the pace and doesn't seem to have much sympathy with those who find it difficult to keep up.

Barnabas has completely different expectations of people. Barnabas will expect people to need encouragement. He will tend to speak up for people so that they're brought into the group much more. He will expect people to progress at different speeds, so he will be happier to slow down until everybody's on board, and then remain watchful for anyone who is flagging a bit at the back. This means that Barnabas is brilliant at working with people who do not make the grade and who have a long way to go in terms of motivation. Barnabas will train people up, having spotted the promise of great things ahead for them; again, exactly as he had done with Paul. You'll have met both these kinds of people at your work, in your family, in your church. You'll instinctively identify with one more than the other.

3. Similar temperaments (why missionaries often don't get on together!)

I was recently speaking at a missionary conference and got chatting with the manager of the conference centre, a fine Christian entrepreneur. At one point in our conversation, which centred on running a Christian conference venue, the manager surreptitiously checked who was around and said to me in low tones 'You know the most difficult weekends we have?' I speculated wildly though hesitated to guess, as one would; but he didn't wait for my answer. He continued (in a hushed voice) 'The most difficult weekends we do are missionary weekends. They're all so strong-willed. They all know exactly what they want. They'll all complain when something's not quite what they expected. They'll all complain when things are too nice! We throw all these people with strong temperaments and definite views together, and it becomes very difficult.'

As in a conference, so on the mission-field.

Paul and Barnabas are both self-starters. They don't need people to tell them what to do. They'll see a situation, assess what needs to be done and they'll get going. They are both passionate men: they feel deeply and strongly and what they feel will direct them, as much as what they think. Paul has a brilliantly logical mind but never let anybody suggest to you that this means that Paul doesn't feel. He demonstrates a thoroughly active emotional life which had become gloriously harnessed to the proclamation of the gospel.

Both men are clear-minded and strong-willed. They are both tough survivors.

4. The rebound effect

After blessing comes . . .

There is a pattern. After the blessings of Kingdom growth, as there had been on Cyprus before John Mark deserted, Satan throws spiritual spanners into the works.

This pattern is found throughout the Scriptures. Men like Paul and Barnabas are true to type among the great figures of the Bible. If it's true for them, it's certainly going to be true for us and this recurring pattern should prepare us, not least by causing us to pray proactively.

We see it as far back in the Bible as Abram's life. In Genesis 12, God says to Abram

> 'I will make you into a great nation
> and I will bless you;
> I will make your name great,
> and you will be a blessing.
> I will bless those who bless you,
> and whoever curses you I will curse;
> and all peoples on earth
> will be blessed through you' (Gen. 12:2–4).

I will make you into a great nation So Abram moves from Haran to the land that God promises: Canaan. He explores the land and, as John Calvin put it in a manner which surely brings out the great reformer's feminine side (!) 'perfumed the land with the fragrance of his faith'. He's been to the great tree of Moreh in Shechem, a focal point for Canaanite religion, and built an altar there. He has pitched his tents east of Bethel, with Bethel on one side and Ai on the other side, two significant religious sites. There again he boldly and defiantly builds an altar to the Lord. Then what happens? Genesis 12:10

> Now there was a famine in the land, and Abram went down to Egypt to live there for a while because the famine was severe. As he was about to enter Egypt, he said to his wife Sarai, 'I know what a beautiful woman you are. When the Egyptians see you, they will say, "This is his wife." Then they will kill me but will let you live. Say you are my sister, so that I will be treated well for your sake and my life will be spared because of you' (Gen. 12:10–11).

So they do so.

> Pharaoh's officials saw her and praised her to Pharaoh, and she was taken into his palace. He treated Abram well for her sake, and Abram acquired sheep and cattle, male and female donkeys, menservants and maidservants, and camels. But the LORD inflicted serious diseases on Pharaoh and his household because of Abram's wife Sarai. So Pharaoh summoned Abram (Gen. 12:14–18).

And pagan Pharaoh has to tell God-blessed Abram the truth and give Abram a lesson in morality. '"Why didn't you tell me she was your wife? Why did you say, 'She is my sister,' so that I took her to be my wife? Now then, here is your wife. Take her and go!"'

After all the blessing and faith, Abram plummets into an unbelieving ruse, jeopardising everything that he's been promised just because he's scared.

Moving on to Moses, we see the same pattern repeating. The first time that Moses shows awareness that he is not an Egyptian but a Hebrew, in Exodus 2, he goes out to see the Hebrew slaves. His heart goes out to them. This young man, who has all the privileges of Pharoah's palace – education, wealth, the best prospects possible lying before him, immediately identifies with the poor and almost sub-human Hebrews. In a moment all the Egyptian baggage, which could easily have held him back, falls away. Instantly it means nothing. But what does he do next? He kills an Egyptian when he thinks that nobody is looking. Ah, but they are. The next day when the two Hebrew slaves challenge him on it, he runs away because he knows the secret is out. He nearly blows the whole thing.

What about Elijah? (By the way, are you remembering who was on the mount of transfiguration with Jesus?) 1 Kings 19:1–4: Elijah has just had the mountain-top experience in which the prophets of Baal are totally humiliated (i.e. Baal is humiliated). His own role as a prophet has been confirmed and exonerated by God. God has glorified himself in great power and majesty.

> Now Ahab told Jezebel everything Elijah had done and how he had killed all the prophets with the sword. So Jezebel sent a messenger to Elijah to say, 'May the gods deal with me, be it ever so severely, if by this time tomorrow I do not make your life like that of one of them.' Elijah was afraid and ran for his life. When he came to Beersheba in Judah, he left his servant there, while he himself went a day's journey into the desert. He came to a broom tree, sat down under it and prayed

that he might die. 'I have had enough, LORD,' he said. 'Take my life; I am no better than my ancestors.'

Elijah runs for his life from 'that woman'. The psychologists would have a field day with that – he was obviously depressed. But the Scriptures don't really present him as a psychological case. Sure, he was maybe tired out, and the Lord feeds him and gives him sleep – classical helps for the depressed. But he is presented to us as somebody who runs away because he's afraid. He runs for his life, he doesn't drag his feet. He sends his servant away. He wants to die. He's had enough: he's gone from the mountain top to the valley bottom.

Think of Peter in Caesarea Philippi. When Jesus asks the disciples 'Who do you think that I am?'

> Simon Peter answered, 'You are the Christ, the Son of the living God.' Jesus replied, 'Blessed are you, Simon son of Jonah, for this was not revealed to you by man, but by my Father in heaven. And I tell you that you are Peter, and on this rock I will build my church, and the gates of Hades will not overcome it. I will give you the keys of the kingdom of heaven; whatever you bind on earth will be bound in heaven, and whatever you loose on earth will be loosed in heaven' (Mt. 16:16).

Absolutely marvellous! Understanding is given through a unique revelation to Peter by the Father, and unique promises are made to Peter by Jesus. Then Jesus explains that 'he must go to Jerusalem and suffer many things at the hand of the elders, chief priests and teachers of the law, and that he must be killed and on the third day be raised to life'. And greatly blessed Peter cannot help himself: 'Peter took him aside and began to rebuke him. "Never, Lord!" he said. "This shall never happen to you!" Jesus turned and said to Peter, "Get behind me, Satan! You are a stumbling-block to me; you do not have in mind the things of God, but the things of men."'

He went from being the rock on which the church would be built to being a stumbling block in the way of the Saviour.

The juxtaposition of Paul and Barnabas being blessed and then failing the One who blessed them recurs in our own lives too. We are made of the same stuff as them and the same devil watches and waits for his moment. He deceives and attacks in order to pull down everything that God has built to his glory. God blesses the church as it shares in his mission and God is glorified. Satan hates God being glorified and so attacks the means by which God is glorified: the church. If he's not attacking with persecution or tribulation from the outside, he will attack with heresy or hatred from the inside.

Who was right?

About Mark? (Probably Barnabas – see how it all worked out)

Without looking through the rest of the story of the church in the New Testament for an answer, would you say Paul was right? After all, John Mark had abandoned them. 'You can't trust a young man like that. It would be irresponsible to take him with you again. You never know what he might do in the future. He's untrust-worthy; he's too much of a risk.'

Or would you be with Barnabas? 'Give the man a second chance. Remember what God did with Jonah? He gave him a second chance to learn God's heart and go to Nineveh. In fact, he gave him a third chance to understand his love for those whom he made. God brings good things out of bad situations.'

Which one would you want, if you were John Mark? If you had deserted in Perga, but now felt ready to go again, who would you want to prevail? Wouldn't you want somebody who would believe in you a bit, believe in God a lot, and give you a second chance? I would.

But whatever the natural inclination of my own mind, the New Testament as a whole indicates that almost certainly Barnabas was right in this case. And it's not Barnabas who tells us he was right, it's Paul. Fast forward to the time when Paul is imprisoned in Rome after that fourth journey across the Med. For two years he's held under house arrest awaiting trial, with the sword of Damocles, as it were, hanging over his head; two years during which many trusted brothers deserted him. Who is it who faithfully and voluntarily shares his imprisonment? It's John Mark. Two out of the four prison epistles, Ephesians, Philippians, Colossians and Philemon, name him.

'My fellow-prisoner Aristarchus sends you his greetings, as does Mark, the cousin of Barnabas' (Col. 4:10), and 'Epaphras, my fellow-prisoner in Christ Jesus, sends you greetings. And so do Mark, Aristarchus, Demas and Luke, my fellow-workers' (Phlm. 23 and 24).

If we take the very last verse in Acts to indicate a limited imprisonment in Rome and that Paul then went off again to revisit the churches, was recaptured and brought back to be imprisoned a second time before being killed, then it is most likely from that second imprisonment in Rome that Paul wrote 2 Timothy 4:9.

> Do your best to come to me quickly, for Demas [who was with him when he wrote to Philemon], because he loved

this world, has deserted me and has gone to Thessalonica. Crescens has gone to Galatia, and Titus to Dalmatia. Only Luke is with me. Get Mark and bring him with you, because he is helpful to me in my ministry.

Recall what had been said about him in Acts 13:5: 'John was with them as their helper.'

The term 'helper' doesn't describe a hanger-on, who tends to get in the way and consume time and resources. It describes someone who serves, who assists, who sees need and ministers to it. It's a technical term and it's a gift of the Spirit, described as 'those able to help others' (1 Cor. 12:28); and it is characteristic of the Spirit himself who, for instance, helps us in prayer – (Rom. 8:26). Helpers are like gold in a fellowship. Mark had this gift: he had showed it when they were setting off on the first missionary journey. And at the end of Paul's life, he still showed it.

There's one other thing that counts in favour of having stuck with John Mark. He wrote the second gospel.

So I reckon that Barnabas was right. There was spiritual gifting and, despite what happened on his first outing, genuine 'stickability' in the lad; he was capable of staying the course.

I also reckon that Paul was big enough to do an about-turn, welcome John Mark back and not only value him personally but also endorse him publicly when he wrote to the church in Colossae and asked for him later on.

Who was right?

About the fall out? (Neither)

They should have done exactly what the council at Jerusalem had done earlier in chapter 15. They should have sat down and worked through the theology of the issue. The council at Jerusalem was rich in theological thinking. They came to terms with a situation that they had not expected, resolved the disagreements and progressed for the sake of the gospel, because they had worked out the theology of the issue. Their answers came from the Bible and from their desire for the gospel to advance in the power of the Spirit. One of the significant things about verses 36 to 40 is the absolute absence of any theologising. Later in his life, Paul would write from prison to the church in Ephesus to say, 'Strive to maintain the unity of the Spirit.' Maybe that fall-out was one of the things that taught Paul how important it was to strive against disunity and to maintain the unity of the Spirit on the basis of the gospel, not to strive with each other without any reference to the gospel. Paul and Barnabas didn't fall out over a matter of doctrine. The essentials of the gospel weren't at issue. There was no threat to spiritual unity from heresy. They could have come to an agreement without either side compromising the truth, since the truth wasn't an issue. But in the heat of the moment, these two men let angry words steal unity and stifle the Spirit.

It takes hard work and a certain amount of warfare against the divided house of Satan to maintain the unity of the Spirit. Neither of them was right over the falling-out. Neither of them could claim to have won.

Who was to be glorified? God

How could God possibly be glorified by this mess?

In the short-term it's immensely sad, but for the long-term: don't panic.

I want to emphasise the sadness of it in order to emphasise the fact that God is glorified. In fact, it is precisely because the situation is so tragic in the short-term that we see the wonder of the glory of God in all this.

Short-term, it is a sad and awful situation, partly because of the qualities of the two individuals, but also because of what they've done together. Think back over what we looked at in the previous two chapters, over what they've been through in the amazing few years that they've been together. What a great partnership the Spirit has forged; what complementary qualities and deep solidarity. They stick their necks out together and suffer persecution together. They preach effectively together; they pray and fast together. And what gracious companionship that allows Barnabas to let Paul take prime position. Such a brilliant partnership would have been known in all the church. Remember how, when they were going from Antioch to Jerusalem for the council at Jerusalem, on the way they kept calling in everywhere, encouraging the saints, telling them what had been happening in Antioch? It's this friendship that's wrenched apart and the shockwaves of their paroxysm would have reverberated throughout the whole church. Tragic.

But when we think longer term the picture begins to change. God is glorified.

In one sense God is glorified because John Mark turns out, by the grace of God, to be a good man. Despite his desertion of the mission and his rejection by Paul, he continues to walk closely with God and stir up his gifts.

But in the bigger picture, God is glorified for another reason. Despite the fall-out, what happens to the gospel? Does the spreading flame of the gospel flicker and die? No. Why is God glorified? Because the advance of the gospel doesn't ultimately depend on the people he is using. He is the Builder. It doesn't ultimately depend on the men and women who are climbing up and down the scaffolding and shifting loads of bricks around and mixing the cement. Ultimately it depends on the One who said, 'I will build my church.' That's why God is glorified.

It sounds counter-intuitive and inside out, from the world's point of view. But we don't look at things from the world's point of view. God is glorified, not by the dispute, which is shameful, don't get me wrong, but by the fact that the gospel progresses, the church grows, and more and more people are saved by his power. Paul would later write to the church in Corinth that the labourer wasn't the important thing. He rebukes them for quarrelling over their factions and celebrity preachers: they are thinking like mere men. Then he writes

> For when one says, 'I follow Paul,' and another, 'I follow Apollos,' are you not mere men? What, after all, is Apollos? And what is Paul? Only servants, through whom you came to believe – as the Lord has assigned to each his task. I planted the seed, Apollos watered it, but God made it grow. So neither he who plants nor he who waters is anything, but only God, who makes things grow (1 Cor. 3:4–7).

Paul, Apollos, Cephas? It didn't really matter. The growth of the building was down to God, not their perfections, after all. That's no excuse for the imperfections. Their fallout was wrong. The gospel did not progress because they fell out, God was not glorified by them falling out. No. The glory of God lies in this: the devil can do his worst and exploit the weaknesses of saints but God still wins. That's why God is glorified. And the worse the devil does (and it wasn't going to get much worse than this in Acts) and the weaker the saints see themselves to be, the greater the glory that God gains.

The significance for us

1. Be wise

Bearing in mind the pattern that we saw from the Old and New Testaments, we need to learn to read the situation that our fellowship or our own lives are in. Is the Lord blessing us? Is the gospel making progress in the lives of non-Christians and Christians alike? Then this is just the kind of situation where the devil loves to throw a spanner in the works. The spanner might arrive through a member of the fellowship, or a set of circumstances or weaknesses that pull someone away from living by faith in Christ's righteousness. Legalism is one spanner in the works; criticism is another, the attraction of alternatives to gathering for worship is another. Satan has a bottomless toolbox full of such spanners. When we're all feeling that things are going well, we have a tendency to be less watchful and our guard drops. We become complacent; we get a bit full of ourselves and the devil comes in with pride.

On fast stretches of dual carriageway with side roads and junctions, there are frequently large signs that warn 'Accident Blackspot'. Read the signs. Read the situation. Look around in the church. You'll have different personality types in your fellowship, with different expectations of the life of the church and of individuals within it. We've also got lots of people of similar temperaments. Be wise. When things are going well, watch out for the devil and pray.

2. Be realistic

What do you expect in church? Some people, by temperament, expect everybody around them to be as near
perfect as they can be. Some of us have to learn to expect
less of people, not because standards ought to drop, but
because we're dealing with people this side of heaven.
Everybody can disappoint you, especially those of
whom you have the highest expectations. Abram,
Moses, Elijah, Peter, Paul and Barnabas disappointed.
Imagine if you'd been getting Prayer Letters from
Moses. You'd be praying away for Moses and pinning
high hopes on him. (He's God's man – and he's got him
right in the centre of Egyptian power. Oh yes, we'll pray
for him.) Then you get a prayer letter from Midian. What
is he doing in Midian? You're answered by the first bullet-point: 'Please pray – I've murdered an Egyptian.' The
second bullet-point doesn't help either: 'The Hebrews
don't want to know me.' Next month comes the really
bad one, still with a Midian postmark: 'Pray on: I could
be here for some time.' Your little prayer group, so opti-
mistic over Moses, is going to have to spend the next
forty years praying for him before he's back in Egypt to
confront the next Pharaoh and lead the Israelites to the
Promised Land.

What does Paul say? 'I am confident of this,' he writes
from prison to the Philippians, 'that he who began a
good work in you will bring it to completion' (Phil. 1:6).
He had no confidence in the Philippians to get themselves completely holy: if he had, he was going to be disappointed. Neither did he expect them to have confidence in him to complete God's work: if he had, they
were going to be disappointed. In the One 'who began a
good work in you' was where his confidence lay for the
work to be brought to completion.

Where do you find your assurance for the future of your fellowship and the progress of the gospel in your area? If it's in your pastor/minister/leadership/vicar, shift it quickly! If hope for the mission of God had been based not on God but on Paul and/or Barnabas, that hope would have lain in tatters by the beginning of Acts 16. Be realistic about people but be equally realistic about God. We're a bunch of sinners thrown together by grace.

3. Be full of patient faith

Do you believe in God's redeeming work? If so, believe long-term. God is very patient with us, not least because he is totally assured of victory; so sure of it that he has told us about it so that we might be full of patient faith, not least concerning each other.

String these three passages together to see the point:

> . . . Christ loved the church and gave himself up for her to make her holy, cleansing her by the washing with water through the word, and to present her to himself as a radiant church, without stain or wrinkle or any other blemish, but holy and blameless (Eph. 5:25–27).

> Once you were alienated from God and were enemies in your minds because of your evil behaviour. But now he has reconciled you by Christ's physical body through death to present you holy in his sight, without blemish and free from accusation (Col. 1:21–22).

> For you know that it was not with perishable things such as silver or gold that you were redeemed from the empty

> way of life handed down to you from your forefathers,
> but with the precious blood of Christ, a lamb without
> blemish or defect (1 Pet. 1:18–19).

That's biblical realism, not pie-eyed naïve optimism. It is
what God has said he will do. Good, eh? Strengthens
your patient faith, does it not?

This assured future not only embraces you and me
individually, it gathers up the whole mission of God to
all the earth. That global mission wasn't going to fail,
even though a greatly blessed partnership crashed and
burned. What does God let John see in Revelation? He
sees the throne room of God in chapters 4 and 5, the
command-centre of the universe; Mission Control. And
there he sees the Lion, like a lamb who was slain, victorious over sin and death, opening the scrolls of God's set
purpose for his church in time and eternity.

> Then one of the elders said to me, 'Do not weep! See, the
> Lion of the tribe of Judah, the Root of David, has tri-
> umphed. He is able to open the scroll and its seven
> seals.' Then I saw a Lamb, looking as if it had been slain,
> standing in the centre of the throne, encircled by the four
> living creatures and the elders . . . And they sang a new
> song: 'You are worthy to take the scroll and to open its
> seals, because you were slain, and with your blood you
> purchased men for God from every tribe and language
> and people and nation (Rev. 5:5–6,9).

He hears, in chapter 11, the loud voices in heaven shouting 'The kingdom of the world has become the kingdom
of our Lord and of his Christ, and he will reign for ever
and ever' (verse 15).

He sees and hears, in chapter 21, the worldwide church
made perfect, and God's voice declaring from the throne

that he and his people are reconciled to unbroken and eternally joyful fellowship. 'I saw the Holy City, the new Jerusalem, coming down out of heaven from God, prepared as a bride beautifully dressed for her husband. And I heard a loud voice from the throne saying, "Now the dwelling of God is with men, and he will live with them. They will be his people, and God himself will be with them and be their God"'(Rev. 21:2,3).

Jesus' prayer for unity in John 17 will be fulfilled in all his people. Your best Christian friend is a sinner. Your church leadership is composed of sinners. You are, in Martin Luther's words, simultaneously just and sinful. Trust the long-term work of the One who will present us all before the Father, spotless, perfect, without any blemishes at all, exactly like Jesus himself. The day will come when Paul and Barnabas, and the countless other fractious, fragmented Christians from down the centuries, will be together again in eternity, singing one song in perfect unity with those from all the earth who have heard the glorious gospel of God.

God is glorified because God wins.

8

What do we expect?

In most responsible jobs there's a certain amount of lee-
way but not much. People's patience soon runs out.
Events beyond your control, your own mistakes, board-
room battles or simply the shifting fortunes of the
marketplace can leave you hung out to dry. But when
Jesus called the most unlikely man on earth to be his witness to the Gentiles, it wasn't a short-term contract that
he had in mind, neither was job tenure dependent on
perfect performance or flawless character. The final outcome of all the work was assured – by God. The fruitfulness of the labourers was certain – because of God.
Patient motivation that would enable the fellow-builders
to endure, would always be generated – from God. The
awful split between Paul and Barnabas threatened to
derail the progress of the gospel, but despite that painful
wrench, the promise of Jesus that his witnesses would go
to the ends of the world still stood.

Undeterred, therefore, and with the commission of the
church, Paul sets out from Antioch again, now with Silas.
This second journey will turn out to be longer and more
costly than anyone had envisaged. It will involve the
spread of the Kingdom of God to Europe. The team will
expand to include, as its most prominent members, Paul,

Silas, Timothy and Luke. Together with such faithful helpers as Priscilla and Aquila, they will form something of a Swiss Army knife, a multi-tool for Kingdom-building: for evangelism and for the strengthening of the Christians in cities and towns throughout the eastern Mediterranean. Paul was no loner. He was a team-player from beginning to end.

God has a vested interest in this kind of teamwork. It points to the shared life and work of Father, Son and Spirit. It speaks volumes for the unity that Christ creates (especially when companions don't fall out!) It powerfully backs up the claim of the gospel to transform humanity. It is a beautiful gift of grace to the poor, the vulnerable and the outcast. It gives a taste of the eternal fellowship of the people of God. In all these ways God is glorified.

How is it in your fellowship?

I want to unpack a few of the stories of God's work through and, principally, in the workers. As he did in Acts 13 and 14, Luke fires off e-mailed memos as the Kingdom advances. We see that the Master-Builder is constantly at work in the lives of his fellow-builders so that he can do his work through them. Just a reminder: God might or might not repeat specific works in your life – this isn't a method to mimic in all its detail. The point is that as we recognise the way that God shapes his fellow-builders' lives in Luke's accounts of what happened, we are better able to read God's work in our own lives. In turn, we become more responsive to him. Attuned to the kind of work that God does so that his workers might do his will, we will, hopefully, be quicker to accept it and work with God.

Great expectations?

But we have to raise a question first if we're going to understand how all this connects with our own lives. In fact, the issue of what we actually expect God's work to be like breaks down into three sets of expectations. We are taught that all three ought to be great expectations.

1. For the Kingdom of God

What do you expect for God's Kingdom as you walk day by day with the King of kings and Lord of lords?

Well, we should expect that the Kingdom will grow; that in its growth it will meet with resistance; and that its growth will be patchy. Its growth was patchy throughout Acts and it always will be. There will always be those who will not want the King, who will turn away as the fickle and self-preserving crowd turned away from Christ and shouted 'Crucify him!' But despite that patchiness, and despite the resistance that the Kingdom meets as it grows by dispelling the darkness of Satan's kingdom, we should expect that the Kingdom will grow.

Why? Because we are inherently good builders? No. Because we have learned really brilliant techniques? No. Because God has promised that the Kingdom will grow. Jesus promised 'I will build my church, and the gates of Hades will not overcome it' (Mt. 16:18). For ages, I had the mental picture of gates flying around all over the place, somehow without harming us. My stupid imagination! It's a picture of a citadel being stormed. 'The gates of Hades will not overcome' means that the gates of hell will not be able to keep the church out or prevent it from plundering Satan's kingdom. According to God's promise concerning his Messiah, 'of the increase of his government and peace there will be no end' (Is. 9:7).

The increase is quantitative (numbers), qualitative (strength) and geographic (places). We need to emphasise all three kinds of growth because one of the recurring points that Luke makes throughout the book of Acts is that the church grew as the word of God spread and it grew in strength, in numbers and in geographical extent. And Luke's important points are the ones that he keeps on making.

We should expect the church to grow through us in all three ways. So where it's being resisted in terms of its numerical growth, does that mean that the Kingdom is not growing? Not at all. In terms of Acts, the fruitfulness of the witness has to do with both the numbers being added to the church and the quality of the church's spiritual life.

We might not think that the Kingdom is growing through us much because so few people are repenting because of us. We are not accustomed to seeing friends, colleagues, families, neighbours etc. repenting right, left and centre and being added daily to the church in their thousands. But we are no less people who belong to the Kingdom of light in the midst of the kingdom of darkness. We are going through that citadel gate and plundering Satan's domain whether by the quantity of the church being added to, or by the quality of the submission and the honour given to the King. The church being strengthened in the faith (the phrase Luke uses in Acts 16:5) represents part of the growth of the Kingdom.

That means that the quality of your discipleship, as much as any conversions that result from your witness, is part of the Kingdom growing. That's not me just trying to give you a nice psychological stroke because you haven't led many people to the Lord recently. Rather, we have to see the growth of the house of the Lord in the terms that the Bible gives us to see it. When a Christian resists temptation, though no-one else sees it, Satan's dark kingdom is being dispelled. When one of us brings their light or 'saltiness' into a difficult moment in the workplace, instead of hiding the life that God has so freely given, Satan is ejected. We are the light of the world, not simply because people come to Christ through us, but because we shine in the darkness by the Christlikeness of our lives.

So if you have been thinking that you're not much of a Kingdom-builder because you haven't led loads of people to Christ, don't think that any more. The numerical growth of the church has always been patchy and is not the only way in which the church grows. All God's children, anywhere and at all times, should be increasing in godliness. What do you expect for the Kingdom when God is at work, which Jesus says he is all the time? Expect it to grow.

2. For the King's fellow-builders?

What do you expect for yourself and your fellow-builders as the Kingdom grows?

Expect the honour of persecution, hardship and trials of one sort or another.

When Paul and Barnabas retraced their steps on the homeward leg of that first journey, they spent time 'strengthening the disciples and encouraging them to remain true to the faith' (Acts 14:22). What did they say? With what kind of half-time motivational pep-talk did they regale the Christians? It's less upbeat than most football managers would ever choose to give. 'We must go through many hardships to enter the Kingdom of God' (verse 22). 'This is the way it's going to be. Don't be surprised, don't feel let down when it's like this. Expect it.'

There's more: on this second journey, Paul and his companions will go to Thessalonica. When he's there, he will tell the new Christians that they're going to suffer affliction, and when he writes to them from Corinth, he reminds them. 'In fact, when we were with you, we kept telling you that we would be persecuted. And it turned out that way, as you well know' (1 Thes. 3:4).

What do you expect when God is at work in you to cause you to do the works of God in an ungodly world? Expect affliction. Wherever the Kingdom is growing, expect trouble. If it's growing qualitatively because you are growing in Christlikeness, anticipate that you will attract hostility and hardship from Satan. It will come in all sorts of ways, through all sorts of people, but don't be surprised that it comes. Expect it.

Another Kingdom-builder, Peter, wrote this

> Dear friends, do not be surprised at the painful trial you are suffering, as though something strange were happening to you. But rejoice that you participate in the sufferings of Christ, so that you may be overjoyed when his glory is revealed. If you are insulted because of the name of Christ, you are blessed, for the Spirit of glory and of God rests on you. If you suffer, it should not be as a murderer or thief of any other kind of criminal, or even as a meddler. However, if you suffer as a Christian, do not be ashamed, but praise God that you bear that name' (1 Pet. 4:12).

So much for 'Cadillac Christianity'! The so-called 'prosperity gospel' promises health, wealth and happiness if you follow Jesus. 'Name and claim your yacht.' 'Dream your second home, size no problem.' It's a sick perversion, a false message, but even so it appeals to materialistic westerners and to impoverished third-worlders alike. It flatly rejects what Jesus taught, contradicting and despising the One who had nowhere to lay his head.

3. For tomorrow?

Maybe it's not what to expect that's our problem. Maybe our problem is that we don't actually 'expect' at all. Maybe we just trundle on through life, one day coming on after another, with no sense of anticipation or expectation of what tomorrow will hold in spiritual terms. I expect that tomorrow this and that will happen. Life is busy, there's work to do, lists abound. I can get through so many days without any explicit expectations of spiritual things, including communicating the gospel or seeing any response to it. It's not that I'm cynically expecting that nothing will happen; it's just that expectation *per se* doesn't often characterise my day. I don't live like that to anything like the extent that the Bible seems to be teaching me to do. I get so busy each day, and there are so many things tomorrow that I'm going to be busy with (you likewise, I'm sure) that spiritual expectations tend to fade away or get drowned out. If I'm going on a mission, or speaking at a conference, then yes, something extraordinary and more obviously 'spiritual' is happening and the expectations rise. But what about the other 95 per cent of life? What about the days, the decades, when we are just 'getting on with life', chasing the shadows of darkness away?

What are your Kingdom expectations for tomorrow? I raise the question simply because it becomes increasingly clear as we go through Acts that the fellow-builders in whom God is working expect 'God stuff' around them. Maybe we do when we're coming to church, as people obviously gathering for a purpose.

Luke's second set of postcards from Philippi, Thessalonica, Berea, Athens and Corinth teach us not to expect a little, but to learn to anticipate and expect that God can do greater things than we might previously have been used to. God can move us up a gear – or several gears.

9

All-consuming passion – more builder's memos

From Philippi
Subject: Flexibility, poise and jail-breaking with God: Acts 16:6–40

This second missionary journey is, like the first, being driven along by the Spirit. The companions sail the trade-winds of God's breath as they are taken away from the obvious route to Ephesus, their intended destination, and travel through the north of the province of Galatia. They are carried to the port of Troas and there Paul experiences, in a dream, the fervent call from a man of Macedonia to come over and help. God frustrated their original plans by closing the doors to Ephesus but he led them by an unexpected route to an unexpected open door: Europe.

For their part, they were able to discern the hand of God and go with the flow. That flexibility proved to be crucial when their ship anchored at the port of Neapolis and the team made their way to the nearby big city of Philippi. There, the customary plan of speaking in the synagogue wouldn't work – not enough Jewish males in

Philippi, so no synagogue. They adapt. That which is not essential moves aside so that the gospel might come through. Finding a place of prayer, down by the river, they share the gospel with a group of women who have gathered there. One of them, Lydia, apparently a successful businesswoman, listens intently. Even though she prays and worships, her heart is still closed to the truth and to God. Until, that is, God does a beautiful thing and 'opens her heart' to Paul's message. As he does so, God opens Europe to the gospel. Europe will never be the same again: we live in both the blessing and the shadow of that moment. We have churches, but the current crisis of spiritual identity in the West also goes back through centuries of conflict between the Kingdom of God and the kingdom of this world to that Saturday morning.

It's after the Lord has laid the first few courses of church bricks, so to speak, that the fun really begins. Read Luke's racy account of the clairvoyant slave-girl, the immoral magistrates and the small matter of an earthquake. It's in Acts 16:16-40.

What the demon-possessed slave-girl is seeing (in verse 18) is absolutely right. So why is Paul unhappy with this? Because he knows that the spirit by which she speaks is not the Spirit of God. By her doctrinally sound shouting she is attaching the gospel to her fortune-telling; but the spirit that allows this woman to recognise the truth prevents her from responding to the truth. She is never going to be delivered to salvation while she is still under the power of this spirit. So after a few days, Paul says 'Enough is enough' and the spirit is cast from her and the way is then cleared, so to speak.

What do we see happening then? First of all, the persecution comes. It has a financial trigger. Greedy people are going to lose some money because of this slave-girl and you can bet your bottom dollar that when the gospel starts hitting people's bank balances, then it will cause persecution. On the surface there's nothing deeply doctrinal about what happens here, nothing profoundly spiritual. This is plain finance. But plain finance is never just plain finance. The finger on the financial trigger is Satan's. Behind the conflict on the streets, there is spiritual warfare in the heavens. The kingdom of this world is being threatened by the Kingdom of God and of his Christ.

If you're a Kingdom-builder in work, you will inevitably introduce Kingdom values into your workplace. They threaten the fiddling, the bending of the rules, the slight massaging of the expenses claim, the exaggeration of the hours for which a customer is billed. They threaten the greed of profit-maximisation. They strike at the root of the attitude that employees are money-making 'units' rather than relational beings made in the image of God. Live a Kingdom life in the temples of Mammon and you can expect trouble. Behind your workplace, as behind the streets of Philippi, the same spiritual warfare rages.

So the losers trump up some false charges. They bring Paul and Silas before the magistrate and claim these men are Jews and are throwing the city into an uproar by advocating customs unlawful for Romans to accept or practise. Oh, please. Who has caused the uproar? Not Paul and Silas. But here's the pattern and privilege of being a Kingdom-builder with Christ. Persecution, false charges, civil unrest, the wrong and unlawful trial. (Roman citizens ought never to have been subjected to this trial, but nobody ever bothered to stop and check first.) In whose steps are they treading? Does it not sound awfully familiar? Christ's experiences are repeated in the lives of his fellow-workers. Expect persecution because the King still challenges the norms of a godless system.

Praising in prison

The persecution lands them in prison and in pain. They have been stripped, humiliated, shamed; they have been beaten, severely flogged. God gave them a vision and they responded in eager obedience. Now they find themselves beaten up and locked in chains. What now of the mission? What now of the purpose of going over to Macedonia?

I ask this because it seems to me that Paul and Silas have had to die to the question 'What's going on?' Their sense of 'things going according to plan' has had to be radically reconfigured from anything like the way the world would think. The amazing part of what's going on is that they don't turn round to God and say 'Lord, you must have made a mistake. Or else we did. Either way, it's not supposed to be like this.' Somewhere along the way they have lost the notion that since they are here for a certain purpose, the mission of God, circumstances must work out smoothly and in a way that makes sense to them. They have let go of the 'Why am I here?' question.

It's no use if those on the building site turn to the Master and say, 'Lord, I'm brilliant at doing windows, so I must do windows. This is my gift, this is my calling. Therefore, with all due respect, Lord,

you must arrange your work accordingly. So what
are you playing at sticking me down here doing the
drains?' Dying to the 'me first' attitude and to our
insecure insistence that we must be able to understand what God is doing, we let God re-cast our
questions. Nonplussed and hurt, as we will be from
time to time, our question to God changes from
'Why?' to 'What's this going to accomplish for the
gospel?'

So they're in prison. But in prison they are full of praise.
'About midnight Paul and Silas were praying and
singing hymns to God, and the other prisoners were listening to them.'

This life with God through the gospel just can't be
kept in! It's got to come out. They witness through their
prayers and their songs. 'Quick, Silas – the other prisoners are listening! Let's sing that new hymn about the
cross. How can we get the last verse to arrive at an
appeal? No – no use. They can't come forward: it's the
chains. How about "My chains fell off"? Yes, that fits.
Let's go for it: after four . . .' They're not ashamed, cowed
or even slightly afflicted by self-pity. In prison, in pain,
with the mission seemingly thrown up in the air they're
praying out loud and joyfully praising God, singing and
witnessing to the other prisoners. (Recall the two questions from the second chapter: if not now, when? If not
here, where?)

Because they have expected persecution they are totally unfazed when it comes. Having died to themselves,
they are totally undaunted by the experience of imprisonment. They rejoice to be given over to death so that
the life of Christ might be revealed in their mortal bodies. 'Make the circumstances worse, guys! Please! That

will make the life of Christ clearer. Make the earthly background darker so that the treasure of the glory of God in the face of Christ might blaze all the more brilliantly.' That's the dynamic. The worse it gets for them, the more mortal they appear to be and the more the life of Jesus is revealed. So Paul writes, a little earlier in 2 Corinthians 4:7,8.

Paul was living by the teaching of Jesus

> Blessed [i.e. happy, fulfilled and contented] are those who are persecuted because of righteousness, for theirs is the Kingdom of heaven. Blessed are you when people insult you, persecute you and falsely say all kinds of evil against you because of me. Rejoice and be glad, because great is your reward in heaven, for in the same way they persecuted the prophets who were before you (Mt. 5:10–12).

Blessed, Lord? Yes, so that the joy might come out. That's what gives Paul and Silas the most amazing poise in the situation. And that poise works out practically. After the earthquake and the prisoners' chains falling off, the jailer realises that he's in more trouble than his life is worth. He is about to kill himself when Paul has the presence of mind to shout and say, 'Don't harm yourself, calm down, we're all OK.' And then he explains the gospel. If he'd been cynical towards God ('Here's another fine mess you've got me into') would Paul have been in an emotional or mental state to see the Kingdom opportunity? Would he have had the poise to react the way he did? And would the Philippian jailer and his family have believed in God?

From Thessalonica
Subject: Jealous opponents and why good builders move on: Acts 17:1–9

Thessalonica was the capital of Macedonia; it's still the second largest city in Greece. There were more Jewish families there than in Philippi, enough for a synagogue. So Paul goes there. If he'd wanted an easy life, he wouldn't have bothered. But despite the likely consequences, he settles in and reasons with them. He takes them through the logical arguments: you really ought to believe in Jesus, because he's the One who fits all the evidence from your own Scriptures.

Predictably there's a backlash of persecution from the Jews. But this time it's fired not by doctrine or by money, but plain old ordinary human (and satanic) jealousy. That's all there is to it. They are simply jealous. Paul, Silas and Timothy are getting more converts than they are. Before God's three musketeers arrived on the scene, these men looked good. But not now. It's so simple, it's almost daft!

If you're good in your workplace, in your family, anywhere in this world, you will provoke jealousy. By living a godly life and commanding respect because of your wisdom and integrity, by not swearing like a trooper and getting drunk at the office party, you will make some people despise you and the gospel simply because they don't have what you've got. You seem to have so much and they have so little. Their lives have gone down the tubes and yours hasn't. They feel shabby because of you. Blend in, and of course you'll be safer. But is that what Kingdom-builders are called to do? Are God's co-workers called to be Christian chameleons?

Not surprisingly, the church grows. 'Some of the Jews were persuaded and joined Paul and Silas, as did a large number of God-fearing Greeks and not a few prominent women' (Acts 17:4). Evangelism and the teaching are going amazingly well. Wonderful work is being done. What opportunities there are for gospel ministry! New-born Christians are soaking up God's word like sponges and facing persecution with mature courage. There's more territory to cover, of course, but that could wait. No one is expecting them back in Antioch by a particular date. Thessalonica is a busy thoroughfare and the strategy of reaching the countryside from the cities would work so well. Why not stay and establish the church in Thessalonica? Surely Paul and his companions need to exemplify endurance here: ride out the storm and persevere?

Well, no. Not at all. Something else emerges for God's fellow-workers to incorporate into their building: the art of moving on. At the instigation of the brothers in Thessalonica, they leave. Timothy will return – Paul is not irresponsible but he can allow the brothers in Thessalonica to be concerned enough for his welfare to send him away.

There's something going on here that has to do with Paul being the most unlikely man in the world. Saul of Tarsus had been a control freak. Paul the apostle trusts God.

Speaking at the Keswick Convention in 2005, Nigel Lee, whose death the following year occasioned much pain amid the thanksgiving for a God-filled life, spoke about this aspect of the work in Acts. With reference to the first missionary journey, he said

> They didn't try to control everything . . . The core truths of the gospel, if properly preached and understood, will

anchor the faith of these young disciples and will go on to shape their whole future growth. This gospel has the power within itself to run and run if allowed to do so. As Paul said, 'It is the power of God unto salvation.'[7]

If we think that we've got to control and command new believers, we're wrong. Saul of Tarsus had lived that way and tried to control what people thought – as he saw it, on behalf of God. That was the role of the Pharisees. He had taken it as a foundational truth for his life that he must make God's people acceptable to God and keep them that way. Unless he and his colleagues were busily controlling the details of his fellow-Jews' lives, God's great enterprise – his people and his Kingdom – would fail.

But on his missionary journeys, Paul and his companions had learned to leave control to God.

From Berea
Subject: The best way to preach and the best way to listen: Acts 17:10–15

What happens when they get to Berea?

They've just seen what trouble can be caused in this part of the world when you go to a synagogue and preach the gospel of Jesus the Christ. So being wise and prudent, they're not going to go anywhere near the synagogue again. They're going to try a different tack. Or . . . 'As soon as it was night, the brothers sent Paul and Silas away to Berea. On arriving there, they went to the Jewish synagogue' (Acts 17:10).

They are bold and courageous as they push back the kingdom of darkness. Far from being passive or merely reactive to the possibilities, they are responsive to Christ and his command. They are not empowered by their own feeble strength, so that they have to go and find the path of least resistance. They are empowered by the Spirit of God, commissioned to go and take on Satan and his kingdom. So they go on the offensive and take on the stronghold. They go straight to the synagogue and preach Christ. The best way to preach is to preach unapologetically and with good courage. Proclamation requires perseverance.

You get a knock-back one day in a seminar, or over tea at home, or on your way into the staffroom. The person that you had a run-in with is going to be there the next day. What do you do? Do you say, 'For the sake of the gospel, I'm going to avoid that person all day long?' What do you do? You persevere with that person from whom the opposition has come. You don't do it in a masochistic way. You don't do it in a way to make yourself obnoxious (I remember a phrase of William Still, my predecessor at the church here in Aberdeen: 'The offence of the cross is inescapable, but the offence of Christians is inexcusable'), but you do persevere. While you're not going to attack that person, you are going to attack the kingdom that that person is captive to, for that person's sake. Target the least likely if you will. Be bold and courageous; take the offensive against the citadel of Satan. It might not turn out as badly as you fear.

So the Bereans don't eat the missionaries. If Paul had been 'twice shy' he would have completely missed the preparatory work that God had been doing in the people of Berea. They were prepared soil, ready for the seed to be planted: they received the message with great eagerness (Acts 17:11). They get out their Scriptures and check

Paul's message. They want to read the references for themselves. If Paul says that the Christ has to die and then rise again on the third day, they want to check it. If that means that Jesus is the Christ, they want to be able to see in the scrolls for themselves that it's true. Paul counts that as a noble thing and commends them. Why? It is because their faith would be stronger. Because Paul, for all that he could pull apostolic rank when necessary in order to get a congregation back into a gospel-guided walk, did not want anybody to build their faith on him. So they do evangelistic Bible studies day after day. And what happens? Many of the Jews believed, as did also a number of prominent Greek women and many Greek men (verse 12).

> Every Kingdom-builder should really want the same. It's not me that you should believe, it's God as he has revealed himself in his word. It's not the ambassador that we want people to follow, it's the King. It's not some celebrity preacher's empire that anybody ought to want to belong to; it's the Kingdom of Jesus Christ.

You'll not believe this, but persecution follows. So Paul leaves. Not because he's scared, but because there are two other Big Apples to pluck. This time there is a positive parting, unlike the one just before this journey started. Silas and Timothy stay in Berea. We know from 1 Thessalonians 3:1ff that Timothy later went back to Thessalonica to strengthen the church there. He would also be able to bring news for Paul of how well they were getting on. Paul moves on to Athens accompanied by the good saints of Berea. It was very nice of them, wasn't it, to escort him right the way to Athens and not leave him unaccompanied on the journey? That kind of loving care speaks volumes for the way in which the Lord had been at work in the lives of these young believers.

From Athens
Subject: Culturally connected preaching to first century postmoderns: Acts 17:16–34

Athens was no longer the great centre of population or the great cultural force that it had once been. Other cities in the Roman Empire were filling those roles when Paul arrived. But the Romans loved everything Greek and in many ways Athens was a sort of touchstone, it was Oxford and Cambridge: not necessarily the best for every subject, but there was something about the name.

Paul actually wanted to go to Rome, not Athens. When he was writing to the church in the Empire's capital, he said that many times he tried to get to Rome but had been prevented. When he and his companions had landed at Neapolis and gone to Philippi, they took the Via Ignatius, which was the main road running east/west across the northern Aegean. Like all other roads, the Via Ignatius led to Rome. Their diversion south may have been prompted by the fact that in Rome the Emperor Claudius was unsympathetic towards Christians and had expelled many of them (including Priscilla and Aquila) along with Jews. For one reason or another, the Spirit who had earlier prevented them from going south in the province of Asia, down to Pisidian Antioch and Galatia and had kept them north, was also keeping them from going to Rome. South-west to Thessalonica, then? Okay, it's still in Macedonia, where the man in the dream was calling from; but to Berea and then even further down to Athens? That's way off the track that they might have expected when they were in Philippi. Yet Athens is an absolutely strategic place. It was still the intellectual high-water mark in people's thinking in the ancient world. So Paul finds himself escorted by the Berean Christians to Athens. They leave him there.

Paul is not a one-man-band. He's a team player, all the time. All the missionary work he has done, he has done with other people. All his apologetic work among the Jewish Christians in Jerusalem, he has done with other people. So his original intention is to wait for Timothy and Silas to rejoin him and then he will begin, with them, the proclamation of the gospel. But something goes on in Paul's heart and mind so that the gospel compulsion that he had received when converted makes the most of the pre-conversion, 'hard-wiring' work of God. The ways that God had made him and re-made him combine in Athens.

God has given Paul an astonishingly good education. He has also given him the ability, as a Roman citizen and a highly educated Greek-speaking Jew, to move between many different cultures. God has also wired Paul so that he works in ideas and doctrines; his analytical mind homes right in on arguments and issues like a heat-seeking missile. But particularly, as a Jew steeped in the law of the Old Testament, Paul has three particular doctrines woven into the fabric of his thinking.

Firstly, there is one God: monotheism. The 'Shema' – 'Hear, O Israel: the LORD our God, the LORD is one' (Deut. 6:4) was the start of the passage from Deuteronomy that every Jew recited throughout their life. Secondly, a four-fold doctrine of creation: God made all things, rules all things, sustains all things and is leading all things towards his end, making all things serve his purpose. Thus we have one God, who is the Creator who, thirdly, has a covenant people for himself, and that covenant is to extend to all nations.

Paul could also adapt his methods wherever he went. He could say, 'I have become all things to all people so that by all means I might save some' (1 Cor. 9:22). The gospel doesn't become all things to all people; the gospel stays exactly the same. But Paul himself had the freedom, in fact a sense of obligation, to be adaptable. He wasn't programmed by habit, or by the rubrics of other Christians.

God has put something else in Paul's life to prepare him for Kingdom-building in Athens. He has given Paul a heart that is absolutely on fire with an all-consuming passion for God, for the gospel and for the Gentiles. So when God plonked him down in Athens, he was like a square peg in a square hole. The fact that he ends up being rejected by the Athenians tells us about their capacity to ignore the truth rather than Paul's supposed incapacity to preach it.

'While Paul was waiting for them in Athens, he was greatly distressed to see that the city was full of idols' (Acts 17:16).

Why was he greatly distressed? Because he'd grown up with a monotheistic background; he'd grown up reciting the Shema from God's word. He saw idol after idol after idol in Athens, and all the teaching from Deuteronomy about idols, all the narrative passages of the Old Testament that taught about the perils of idolatry, all that's in the prophets lambasting idolatry and the exile to cure God's people of their idolatry; all of it flooded his mind and heart. This one God had saved him by his grace, forgiven his sin, clothed him with righteousness – this One God is glorious and Paul doesn't want the glory going to other gods. And these people were wasting their lives seeking the one true God in the pathetically inadequate spare-parts bins of polytheistic pick-and-mix spirituality. He couldn't sit comfortably with it; it deeply distressed him. He was provoked, irritated, upset. In fact, 'greatly distressed' translates the same Greek word that described the row, the paroxysm, that had flared up between him and Barnabas. This is a better paroxysm!

I've been a Christian for thirty-four years. In these years I've been privileged to receive excellent teaching, to watch outstanding examples, to read books, listen to sermons, go on missions (beach missions, park missions, market-square missions on soap boxes) and minister the gospel. Yet I don't think I'm half as bothered by the idolising of wealth and pleasure around me in Aberdeen as Paul was by the idolatry that he saw in Athens. He could not sit comfortably in a city like that. What are we playing at?

But Paul didn't just have an Old Testament background. He had that heart for God and for the gospel and for the Gentiles. A good Jew in Athens, seeing all the idolatry, would say, 'I'm not going to touch these Athenians, Gentile dogs that they are.' But Paul, instead of standing right back and saying, 'What a disgusting lot these Athenians are!' engages. He wants to win them.

Even though he's a team-player, he can't wait for Silas and Timothy to join him. He can't just sit there with nothing being said, with nothing about the truth of Jesus Christ being presented to rescue people from their idolatry. 'So he reasoned in the synagogue with the Jews and the God-fearing Greeks, as well as in the market-place day by day with those who happened to be there' (Acts 17:17).

He would go and reason with anybody who was there. The Agora was a huge market square in Athens, with colonnades round it that created shady areas. In the cool comfort of these colonnades were shops and spaces for meetings and debates and long conversations about the latest intellectual fashions. So Paul went there, and whoever he met he would speak to, reason with, engage them with the truth of the gospel. He falls into a debate with some of the Athenian intellectuals: 'A group of Epicurean and Stoic philosophers began to dispute with him. Some of them asked, "What is this babbler trying to say?" Others remarked, "He seems to be advocating foreign gods." They said this because Paul was preaching the good news about Jesus and the resurrection' (Acts 17:18).[8]

It's very contemporary. If we had a questionnaire with two columns with symptoms of being an Epicurean on one side and symptoms of being a Stoic on the other, and we asked people the right questions, we would get box after box after box ticked in predominantly one or the other column. We live now in an age where people will cope with the human condition and try and account for it by doing anything and everything except turning to the God of the Bible. By and large people will go for either pleasure (the Epicureans) or reason (the Stoics). And by and large, people will go for all sorts of gods (just pick your own) or will believe that God is just a word for the world and its spirit. We are surrounded by Epicureans and Stoics. Culturally speaking, our century and Paul's century have never been as close as they are now.

Paul meets them on their own turf. He does not change the gospel to make it attractive to them, as we will see;

but he is going engage with them so that he can communicate the gospel. In Athens, just as much as anywhere else, he is being all things to all people so that by all means he might win some.

Some call Paul a babbler. (It's a word that meant someone who picks up ideas and trades in them. It was originally used for birds pecking at seed; pecking at ideas and peddling them cheaply.) Others say that he seems to be advocating foreign gods. They mishear Paul use the word *anastasis*, which is the Greek word for resurrection; it sounds like Anastases, a woman's name. They thought, 'Is Anastases this God's wife?' But as he continues with them, they turn a little bit antagonistic. So they take him to the Areopagus where they can find out more.

Underneath the surface, something else is going on. First of all, this thing about foreign gods. Historically, among the philosophers, foreign gods were bad apples. Socrates had been charged with introducing foreign gods. A couple of centuries before Paul, a priestess had been stoned to death in Athens for introducing foreign gods. So 'he seems to be advocating foreign gods' is not an innocent little phrase. It's "Ello, 'ello, 'ello; there's a crime going on here.' Also, any Greek-speaking readers of Acts would recognise the phrase, 'they took him and brought him to a meeting of the Areopagus', as being exactly what they did to Socrates, the greatest and wisest of all the Greeks.

The Areopagus was originally a place, the hill of Ares; in Latin it was known as Mars Hill. By Paul's day, the Areopagus was the name given to the council that had originally met there. When Paul was dragged before it, the council met in the colonnade round the edge of the Agora. They were the Thought Police in Athens. If Paul was to preach in the city, he had to be accredited by them. Paul is being brought before the Areopagus with a big question mark over his head. Is he an agitator, a dangerous subversive, a stirrer?

How will Paul speak to them? Surprise, surprise: he comes straight out with the gospel. They put his head in the lion's mouth and he says 'Right, while it's in here, I might as well preach the gospel!'

He begins politely: they're sophisticated intellectuals – they respond to a bit of civilised flattery. He wants to win a hearing. 'Men of Athens!' (The Areopagus was male and there would be very few women around. Damaris is mentioned almost certainly because it was unusual for a woman to be in the Agora taking part in a debate. Even educated women in Athens were looked upon as tenth class citizens by the Greek intelligentsia.) 'I see that in every way you are very religious. For as I walked around and looked carefully at your objects of worship, I even found an altar with this inscription: TO AN UNKNOWN GOD.'

There were several statues to unknown gods in Athens. It dates back almost certainly to the time of great trouble, to the earthquake in Athens. To make sure you appeased every god, you built a statue to one that you didn't know about, just in case it might send another quake. It was a way to hedge your celestial bets.

Then Paul begins to unfold the gospel to them. Recall that Paul was steeped in the Old Testament; watch how he works with the doctrine of creation with these Athenians.

> The God who made the world and everything in it is the Lord of heaven and earth and does not live in temples built by hands. And he is not served by human hands, as if he needed anything, because he himself gives all life and breath and everything else. From one man he made

all the nations, that they should inhabit the whole earth; and he determined the times set for them and the exact places where they should live. God did this so that they would seek him and perhaps reach out for him and find him, though he is not far from each one of us. For in him we live and move and have our being. As some of your own poets have said, 'We are his offspring.'

He made us all. He is Lord of all. We don't sustain him by taking him offerings in a temple: he sustains us. It's all wonderfully appropriate because it's the connecting point with these people. Here is something that they can understand, that Paul can speak to them about on their own terms. 'Listen, you believe X about these crucial things, but Y is actually the case. Your poets agree with me. But this God isn't remote and uninterested: he wants us to know him. He's not an unknown god. He has revealed himself to us, and he wants us to seek him and perhaps reach out for him and find him.'

Then he finds another contact point: the Stoics believed that God was all around you. So Paul says God is not far from each one of us. And another: the Stoics believed that we were all part of God's family and we were all God's children. Paul is prepared to say, 'Yes, in one sense we are.' We are his offspring. Therefore, we owe him, therefore don't try and be god over him but repent. Turn from the idolatry and turn to him because the One he raised from the dead will be your Judge, having power over death and life.

Paul finds the points of contact with the people that are listening, and completely challenges everything they think about God, about themselves, about eternal life. What is the result? 'When they heard about the resurrection of the dead, some of them sneered, but others said, "We want to hear you again on this subject." (The

Epicureans would sneer because they believed that once
you died that was it, which is why you had to live as
enjoyable a life as possible: stack in all the pleasure now
because once you died there was nothing else.)

That sounds promising, but actually it isn't.
Remember the situation. Paul has been hauled before
them so that they can decide whether or not he can go on
preaching in Athens. What is the outcome? Some of
them sneer and some of them say, 'We'll hear you again
on this.' They're politely saying 'No, I don't think so.'

But a few believed. A few men became followers of
Paul and believed. Among them was a member of the
Areopagus, Dionysius. We could not possibly underestimate the significance of the gospel reaching that one
man in the Areopagus. Also a woman named Damaris
and a number of others responded.

So Paul had to leave Athens. He wasn't going to get
the licence to preach. He was being turned away. At least
he could trust the few who had come to faith to God.

New fields lay ahead. He made his way down to
Corinth.

Challenging, isn't it? Kingdom-builders are sent
where people are, to understand what they think and
engage them in their own terms without altering the
gospel. Then we have to lead them to the crunch:
accept or reject Christ's forgiveness; make sure
you're ready for the coming Judge.

We have to ask ourselves, how do our churches do
that and how do we do that each day? Do we expect
everybody to come in to where we are and listen to
us on our terms so that they might be won? That's
not what Paul was doing. He went to where they
were, spoke to them in their terms and presented the

gospel. We could do that, when we go to work and when we spend time with other people outside church. God is sending us to engage all the time. But do we actually engage? Do we understand how Dave and Sarah really think? We've been stuck in our Christian worlds for so long that our minds work differently, even our language is different. Do we really know how they perceive us, or what they think if we say 'God'? What goes on in Dave's mind when I say 'sin'? If you say to Sarah, as you stand at the sink in the staffroom, that you've been saved, what will she actually hear? And if we do try to engage with people and get inside their minds, how can we do it without changing the gospel, and how can we do it better? We cannot effectively reach out until we know those to whom we are speaking; and to know them we must ask the right questions about them and listen carefully to the answers.

From Corinth
Subject: Encouraged by friends, loved by Jesus: Acts 18:1–14

There is much about Paul's time at Corinth that has a strategic significance for the proclamation of the gospel. For instance, Gallio, the Roman proconsul over the whole province, effectively rules that since the Jews' problem with Paul is merely an internal difficulty within a legally recognised religion, the law has no place to stop him from preaching. This gives Paul great freedom to declare the truth.

But there is something else that has to do with the way in which God handles his fellow-builders.

When Paul gets to Corinth, alone, he forms a partnership with Priscilla and Aquila; tentmakers who had been expelled from Rome along with the others that Claudius had considered dangerous to good civil order. Trades were not as internally competitive then as they are now. They formed guilds and looked out for one another. All the guilds had their own feasts, their own gods, their own shrines. If you were part of the tentmakers' guild you were expected to go in for all the accompanying idolatry. So if you're a Christian tentmaker and you found another Christian tentmaker, wow! That was wonderful and promised real fellowship and companionship. You'd work long hours with them, talk a lot with them and strengthen one another.

You know what it's like when you've been the only Christian in a workplace and then another Christian comes and joins you in that workplace. I spent seven years at Batley Boys Grammar School, and when I was in the sixth form, there were only four Christians in a school of 540 boys. It was absolutely great to have three other Christians around; we would meet up sometimes at morning break, just for ten minutes in a tiny room, for a short Bible reading and to pray for one another, and then off. Brief, but what an encouragement it was. If there are only a few other believers around where you work, meet up with them. Don't form a little holy huddle that self-righteously keeps the gospel to itself and never wants an 'outsider' to come in, but do encourage one another.

What we see in Corinth is the wonderfully sustaining effect of partnership in the gospel.

There he met a Jew named Aquila, a native of Pontus, who had recently come from Italy with his wife Priscilla, because Claudius had ordered all the Jews to leave Rome. Paul went to see them and because he was tent-maker as they were, he stayed and worked with them. Every Sabbath he reasoned in the synagogue, trying to persuade Jews and Greeks. When Silas and Timothy came from Macedonia, Paul devoted himself exclus-ively[9] to preaching, testifying to the Jews that Jesus was the Christ (Acts 18:2–5).

Remember what's happened to Paul. He was flogged and imprisoned in Philippi, persecuted and hounded by his own people the Jews in Thessalonica and Berea, and shut out of Athens.

Do you think he bounced into Corinth full of the joys of Christian service? I don't think so. I think Paul arrived in Corinth as flat as a pancake, tired and probably still physically suffering from the beatings and floggings he received in Philippi. These were arduous journeys which left him exhausted and despondent. 'When I came to you, brothers, I did not come with eloquence or superior wisdom as I proclaimed to you the testimony about Christ' (1 Cor. 2:1). He was trembling and weak, as we read in what he later wrote to the church in Corinth: 'I came to you in weakness and fear '(1 Cor. 2:3).

Meeting Aquila and Priscilla and then being reunited with Silas and Timothy and hearing the good news about the Thessalonians must have heartened him tremendously.

But even this was not enough. He needed something else. He must have done, because Jesus gave him some-thing else. It is one of the wonderful and deeply moving moments in Paul's ministry. Jesus isn't just a figure in a gospel message. He isn't just a character, a name in a system of thought. Jesus is a real person. This real person does for his fellow-builder what nobody else could do. Jesus visits him in the night-time, when he is alone. He speaks to him one-to-one, strengthens him with heaven's strength and puts fresh courage into him; he gets him back on his feet and helps him to persevere. Verse 9: 'One night the Lord spoke to Paul in a vision: "Do not be afraid . . ."'

Jesus comes to him saying, 'Don't be afraid.' You only say that to people who are afraid, don't you? 'Don't be afraid?' Afraid of what? Afraid of them? Afraid of the opposition? Afraid of failing? Don't be afraid. Keep on speaking. Do not be silent. It's costing you, Paul. It's costing me. It's easy to be silent, but don't be. Keep on speaking. And here comes the Old Testament phrase to this man who is steeped in the Old Testament, this phrase which was used when the people were leaving Egypt, or when armies were going into battle, or when individuals faced terror or loneliness: 'I am with you.' They can do what they like, but I am with you. Bigger than them, stronger than them, better than them. 'And no one is going to attack and harm you, because I have many people in this city.'

What a Lord, who comes to us at the moment when we're low enough to give up and when mere human companionship, however good, is not enough. What a kind Lord to strengthen and sustain his weary and embattled friend. And it worked! 'So Paul stayed for a year and a half, teaching them the word of God' (verse 11).

It is a most wonderful, personal, pastoral ministry of Jesus, who feels our pain with us and has gone through it before us. Paul is like the prophet Jeremiah in some ways. There's a passage in his book which just puts it all together very helpfully: Jeremiah 20:8ff. Here is persecution: 'The word of the LORD had brought me insult and reproach all day long.'

That's exactly Paul's experience. The word of the Lord, so vital for the growth of the Kingdom, has brought him 'insult and reproach all day long'. But Jeremiah, just like Paul in Athens, could not sit there without saying something. He had to speak. Here is persistent proclamation: 'But if I say, "I will not mention him or speak any more in his name," his word is in my heart like a fire, a fire shut up in my bones. I am weary of holding it in; indeed, I cannot' (Jer. 20:9).

And that brings conspiracy and more persecution from his own countrymen, just as it had for Paul in Philippi, Thessalonica and Berea: 'I hear many whispering, "Terror on every side! Report him! Let's report him!" All my friends are waiting for me to slip, saying, "Perhaps he will be deceived; then we will prevail over him and take our revenge on him"'(Jer. 20:10).

Yet God was with Jeremiah as he was with Paul that night in Corinth, to give him strength, to pastor him and help him to endure: 'But the LORD is with me like a mighty warrior; so my persecutors will stumble and not prevail. They will fail and be thoroughly disgraced; their dishonour will never be forgotten' (Jer. 20:11).

How does God work in the lives of his fellow-builders to keep them going? The Lord Jesus comes to us with an intimacy that nobody else can manage, in order to pick us up and put new heart into us; to send us back out revitalised simply because he is with us. And no matter what people try, it's not going to bring any harm to us ultimately, neither is it going to stop God's mission. Where are you now, emotionally, physically? Exhausted, spent, afraid? Ask him to pastor you. Turn to the Physician of your soul. Find a quiet place and wait for him to minister to you.

10

Signing off – an all-consuming passion

The rest of the journey is dealt with quickly by Luke. Paul and his friends leave Corinth eventually, and travel to Ephesus. He parts with Priscilla and Aquila and briefly engages with the Jews in the synagogue, promising that he will return if it was God's will. He sails to Caesarea and from there goes up to Jerusalem, to fulfil his Nazirite vow at the Temple, and from there he travels north again, back to base at Antioch.

But Paul can't stay in Antioch. He has an inner compulsion to leave; so after a while there he goes on his third journey, around all the places that he visited on the first one and to the places that he couldn't get to on the second one because the Lord was diverting him to Europe. This time, the Lord doesn't stop him; Paul visits the churches, strengthening the saints. He can't stop building up the church. He just cannot stop spreading the word of God.

What has happened by the end of the second journey? It has been such an all-encompassing experience that it has fixed Paul's heart on the building of God's Kingdom. God has, as it were, entirely reconfigured his

one-time enemy. Once, this proud Jew persecuted
Christ. Now he will spend all his energies glorifying him
by making him known. It's no longer a task. It's his life,
and one day it will be his death.

There's a passage in which Paul describes this himself. Philippians 2:17 – 18; 'But even if I am being poured
out like a drink offering on the sacrifice and service coming for your faith, I am glad and rejoice with all of you.
So you too should be glad and rejoice with me.'

Paul paints a picture of the offerings in the Old
Testament. The meat-offering is placed on the altar and
as it's burning up, an extra offering, the drink offering,
was poured out on top. It was extra sacrifice that people
added just because they were so thrilled with God. It
was an extravagant and, strictly speaking, unnecessary
gesture of love and devotion.

Paul is saying: 'If my life is being poured out like that
onto the sacrifice of your lives, if we are being consumed
with devotion to God, that's cause for rejoicing for me.'

Paul has an all-consuming passion for God. It is right
at the heart of what it means to be a Christian. Peter,
Stephen, Philip, Paul: these fellow-builders couldn't fit
their service for God neatly into an otherwise undis-
turbed world. God was everything to them. He was why
they lived; he was why they got up in the morning; he
was how they managed to get to sleep at night when
they slept or how they could sing praise at midnight in
a prison. He was why they would die for the sake of the
gospel. They felt God passionately. So it didn't matter
what people did to them. In fact, the worse it got, the
more pleased they were, because the more they died, the
more Christ was revealed.

This is not a carnal passion. Some people are naturally
and intensely passionate; others have all the emotional
intensity of a turnip, they don't get worked up over

anything, ever. It's just the way they are made. But this passion for God comes from God.

It was God that put the passion in Paul's heart. Only God could change the most unlikely man on earth into such a fellow-builder, for only God has such a zeal for his own glory. He is rightly passionate for his honour, for his Kingdom to grow, for sinners to be saved. He is moved by people's plight. He is moved by people's prayers. He feels for sinners in their separation from him. He longs for his house to be built. He is fervent about glorifying his Son; he is totally committed to the eternal life of the church. Of Christ it was said: 'Zeal for your house has consumed me.'

Does anything about the building of God's house consume us? Is there any of God's passion for his own glory and for his Kingdom coursing through our spiritual veins? May God give us this; then we'll be prepared to die to self and we'll be the better Kingdom-builders for it; and if these two books have done anything to cause us to ask for such all-consuming passion, then they will have been worth it.

Endnotes

1 Smart, D., *Kingdom Builders* (Milton Keynes: Authentic Media, 2005).

2 Cranfield, C.E.B., *The Epistle to the Romans Vol. II* (Edinburgh: T&T Clark, 1979), p. 534.

3 Levi, P., *If Not Now, When?* (London: Penguin Books, 2000). The title comes from the work of a Jewish rabbi who died in the year that Jesus was probably born. The controversies between his followers and those of the more conservative and strict Rabbi Shimmel create a large part of the backdrop to some of Jesus' exchanges with the scribes and the Pharisees. Hillel was a wise teacher. Some of his sayings became part of a collection called *Pirkei Avot – The Sayings of the Fathers*. (It's sometimes referred to as *The Ethics of the Fathers*, since they are practical snippets collected in order to indicate how to behave well. In them, Hillel says, 'If I am not for myself, then who will be for me? And if I am only for myself, then what am I? And if not now, when?')

4 Kelly, G., *Six Habits of a Highly Connected People* (Milton Keynes: Spring Harvest Publishing Division/Authentic Media, 2003).

5 Jeffrey, T. and S. Chalke, *Connect!* (Milton Keynes: Spring Harvest Publishing Division/Authentic Media, 2003).

6 He's still around: Hermes has been either promoted or demoted, depending on how you look at it, to become the symbol of the Greek Post Office. So as he delivers letters, perhaps the god with the winged cap rescues present-day posties from Greek hounds with fanged teeth. Nice.

7 You can read Nigel's talk and many others from the 2005 Convention in Hull, A., ed., *The Glory of the Gospel* (Milton Keynes: Authentic Media, 2005).

8 Who were the Epicureans and Stoics? Epicureanism was a school of Greek philosophy which went back to Epicurus (not surprisingly), who lived from 342 to 270 BC. The Epicureans believed that we live for pleasure; they were hedonists. Our proper aim is to enjoy a good, pain-free life with little or no distress. They were polytheists; that is, they believed that there were many gods. In fact they believed in the whole range of Greek gods. But they believed that the gods weren't very interested in our lives and we could get on without their interference. The Stoics traced themselves back to the Cypriot philosopher Zeno, who lived at the same time as Epicurus, 340 to 265 BC. They could hardly have been more different from the Epicureans. The Stoics didn't believe that pleasure was the greatest good in life: in fact, they were down on pleasure. They were pantheists; that is they believed God was in everything, that God was really another name for the whole world's soul. They believed that God was in trees and plants and animals and rocks and babbling brooks and all nature. They were also rationalists who believed in the power of logic to provide certainty. They were strongly committed to the self-sufficiency of the individual, which is why we call people stoical. We aren't saying they are pantheists; we are saying that they have got grit and determination and they just seem to get themselves through troubles. They're not going to crumple; they don't let their emotions get the better of them. Stoics believed that we

have the resources within ourselves to get through any kind of situation. You can cope. Starch your upper lip into quiver-free stiffness and reason your way out of a problem. Victorian England was full of unofficial stoics. They were the two great rival schools in Athens: the two rival ways of accounting for the world and coping with life. They were also both novelty-seekers: both the Epicureans and the Stoics were constantly looking for new ideas, new philosophies, to examine. They were both completely at odds with everything in the gospel that Paul believed so passionately.

[9] Literally, he 'held himself to'.